MW00860845

The Seasonal Gardener

Anna Pavord

The Seasonal Gardener

Creative Planting Combinations

Anna Pavord

PREFACE

The Seasonal Gardener is an extensively reworked edition of another book, *Plant Partners*, that I wrote some twenty years ago. The central idea is the same: sixty of my favourite plants are presented together with companions that will make them sing. The four sections follow the flowering year, from the hellebores and snowdrops of winter and early spring to the cyclamen and salvias of autumn.

The original book featured only herbaceous plants, annuals and bulbs. This edition includes some of the superb shrubs that have gradually become the focus of my own gardening style over the last couple of decades. How, I think now, could I ever have lived without the scent of daphnes, or the magnificent foliage of a shrubby peony such as *Paeonia delavayi*? Shrubs add bulk and substance to a garden. They give their own dramatic performance in season, but they also provide a generous backdrop to other more ephemeral plants around them. In choosing twenty of my favourite shrubs to star in this book, form and foliage have been as much in my mind as flowers.

There has also perhaps been a change in the way we look at our gardens, a shift reflected in this gorgeously illustrated new edition. We are now much more aware than we used to be of the masses of creatures that need and use our gardens much more than we do. This is especially true of the insects that feed as happily on the flowers of an ornamental allium as they might once have done on the buttercups of our fast-disappearing meadows. Many of us now garden in a looser, less controlling way than we used to. Changes in gardening style since the original publication of *Plant Partners* in 2001 have introduced us to previously unfamiliar plants, including grasses and a burgeoning range of late-season salvias, which have now found a place in *The Seasonal Gardener*.

In the last twenty years too, I have fallen in love with a host of new plants. *Crocosmia* 'Lucifer', a long-standing favourite of mine, has now been supplanted by 'Hellfire', which is even more fiery and magnificent. Among the catmints (*Nepeta*), I've found 'Walker's Low' a much more accommodating garden plant than 'Six Hill's Giant', an earlier favourite. Both find a place in the present cavalcade of planting ideas.

Among gardeners, as with fashionistas, what goes with what will always be a matter of debate. But this book can start you on a glorious new voyage of discovery, as season follows season. I very much hope you will enjoy it.

ANNA PAVORD

INTRODUCTION

Our gardens provide us with a curious combination of constancy and change. They surround and ground us with their familiar landmarks but at the same time excite us with their endlessly shifting elements. The biggest transformations, of course, are brought about by the seasonal moves of spring into summer, summer into autumn, autumn into winter.

This book, arranged in four chapters, is about ways of grouping plants in a garden to give you a generous display through those seasons – from the longed-for snouts of aconites (*Eranthis*) pushing through the ground in late winter to the brilliantly vibrant seed heads of spindle (*Euonymus*) lighting up an autumn dusk. Sixty star plants are featured in the following pages, each presented with a supporting cast: two other plants that will provide the best kind of companionship for it. Sometimes the supporting plants will perform at the same time as the star to deliver a Grand Slam seasonal show. In other groups, companions are chosen to fill in the gaps when the star is 'resting' or having an off season. The spring-flowering *Narcissus* 'Thalia', for instance, is one of the supporting cast suggested in the High Summer chapter for the star plant *Thalictrum delavayi* 'Hewitt's Double' (see p.154). The other supporting plant here is a grass, *Molinia*. Both thalictrum and molinia are late-season plants; the narcissus can be spread about to bring delight to that place in spring.

This is the decision you have to make when you are putting groups of plants together in the garden. Are you intent on maximum impact, with everything coming out together at a particular time? Or are you planting for continuity, so that whenever you look at a particular spot, something good is happening there? Bulbs (as with *Narcissus* 'Thalia') are particularly useful in bringing an extra spring explosion to a group primarily planted for a later season. With a little experience, you soon learn who your best friends are, for there are some plants, notably hellebores and euphorbias, that contribute to the garden all the year round. If you include one or two of these 'bankers' in your plant groups – plants that you can bank on under most circumstances – you will be more than half way to success.

The best bankers have good foliage, because in the end it is leaves, not flowers, that make your garden feel rich, abundant and well-furnished. In most groups in this book, you will find at least one plant that will continue to have impact when its flowers have finished. By choosing star plants from each seasonal section, you will ensure that your garden does not run out of steam by the middle of summer, and that there will be plenty more treats to come. Gradually, you will begin to see how you can link different trios of plants to spread their delights over a whole bed – plants such as the groundcovering ferns suggested in the spring section, joining hands seamlessly with an early summer group such as dicentra, anemone and hosta (see p.66) to create a patch where there is always something to delight.

The groups of plants suggested here give you a starting point, but some of them, especially annual flowers such as marigolds and love-in-a-mist, will have their own ideas about where they would like to be and what tricks they would like to show you. The whole *raison d'être* of an annual is to grow, flower and set seed in a single year. This self-seeding can be a boon to a gardener, since combinations spring up that you might never have imagined yourself. Of course, you, the gardener, will be editing the scene, but over time, with the help of self-seeding plants, you may find that your garden drifts towards a looser, more relaxed style, more in tune with the natural world.

In this cavalcade of marigolds and nasturtiums, hellebores and hostas, daylilies and irises, tulips and spurges, you will not find any trees, though I have introduced some of my favourite shrubs. Every garden needs both trees and shrubs to give bulk and presence, as well as shade and a sense of permanence in a plot, but the planting schemes in these pages are made up chiefly of perennials, biennials, annuals and bulbs. It is what we have most of in our gardens, and with them we can create a host of varied, seasonal delights. In a small garden, there may be room for only one tree, but under and around it you can build up a year-long display of shrubs, perennials and other smaller plants, mixing and matching the combinations I suggest in the following pages.

Because plants are living things, extremely responsive to factors such as rain or the lack of it, sun, frost and air temperature, flowering times may fluctuate from one year to the next. Aspect also has an effect on performance, as does soil. Heavy clay soils are slower to warm up in spring than light, sandy ones, so plants may be later in waking up. In this book, plants have been nudged into particular seasons, but they do not necessarily stick to the plot. The spring season is particularly difficult to predict, as a mild winter or a series of harsh frosts can advance or retard flowering a good deal. Frost might bring a sudden end to your late summer display too, but these minor hiccups should not prevent you from continually daring yourself to try something different: zinnias instead of dahlias or tithonias instead of tobacco plants.

There has never been a time when gardeners have had more plants to play with than we have now, but just having them is not enough. The whole point of gardening is to think about our plants' needs and then, by placing them in good company, to make them shine as brightly as they are able, for as long as possible. Get into the habit of looking ahead. Your spring display may be fantastic (spring usually is), but what show-stopper can you put in place to take over later in the season? You will find plenty of suggestions in the following pages. Watch what the plants want to do, where they spread themselves, and learn from that. Loosen the bonds. Think wild. There may be a corner of your lawn where you can introduce scillas or delicate mauve *Crocus tommasinianus* to flower in the grass in spring. In early autumn, plant snowdrops, camassias and lovely pheasant's eye daffodil (*Narcissus poeticus* var. *recurvus*) in a spare piece of ground and scatter a fine grass seed mix over the same spot. Spring will bring a Botticelli vision to your own back garden. There are no rules here, but many ravishing possibilities.

I

Signs of Spring

It is, of course, perfectly possible to write lyrical words on the garden in winter: silhouettes of trees against the darkening sky, white chalice buds of snowdrop, choirboy-ruffed aconites, all that sort of thing. But the winter garden – who needs it? First of all, there is the dressing up: double rations of socks, Wellington boots, coat, hat, thick gloves. And that is not allowing for rain, or opening the back door to have it snatched out of your hand by a 75-mile-an-hour gale. Then there are the pleasures of hail, a sensation like being peppered with iced ball bearings, watching as the stuff piles up inside the rosettes of foxglove leaves like ice cream in a cone.

You can only stay positive for so long. By the time you have stubbed your toe on an icy edging stone while trying to smell a primrose, by the time you have skated over the quagmire of your lawn and viewed the sodden wastes of your borders, where rubble seems to be mysteriously bubbling up as if from an underground landfill, you may have decided that the pleasures of the winter garden are only for masochists. The leaves of gunnera, hanging in this season like rhinoceros skins, seem to say the same thing.

The ground could not look more unappealing: heavy, sullen, sticky, cold. The thought of getting your hands in it is as appetizing as dallying in cold porridge. The eye rests on dead fern fronds, the sticks of summer roses and melted puddles of crinum foliage. If you must have a winter garden, make it one that you can plant in summer and then view from the comfort of a centrally heated perch indoors. Any winter effects need to be right outside a window. It is hopeless having winter plantings dotted randomly round the garden where they sit as lonely as penguins on a broken ice floe and finding them means suffering terminal frostbite.

You might think of bringing winter plants together, for instance under the canopy of a beech or some similar deciduous tree. In winter, when the branches are bare, the ground underneath gets more light and moisture than at any other time of the year. You might start with a big, dark *Helleborus foetidus* (see p.178) – even better, a group of them. By adding some spreads of white snowdrop (*Galanthus*; p.30, p.84) and yellow aconite (*Eranthis hyemalis*; see p.68) around their feet, you can imagine quite a pleasant winter scene developing. It would also be a good way of using this kind of ground. It is difficult to get anything special going under big trees in summer, because the earth becomes so dry and shaded. The hellebores, being sculptural evergreen plants, would continue to contribute, however; you might add small wild daffodils to carry on through the spring, with woodruff or some equally forgiving groundcover to take over later. The woodruff (*Galium odoratum*; see p.72) has tiny cross-shaped flowers scattered over mats of foliage that is as finely cut as mossy saxifrage.

For maximum impact, of course, you want groups of plants coming to a peak at the same time in various parts of the garden, but because gardens now are mostly smallish, the schemes also have to go on working, even if in a less concentrated way, for the rest of the year. This is particularly so with groups of winter plants, which is why it is worth persevering with one or two summer additions, without losing sight of the fact that the patch's main contribution will be a winter one. You may find the position too dry for the woodruff, which flowers in late spring and early summer, and reach instead for golden-leaved creeping Jenny (*Lysimachia nummularia* 'Aurea') as groundcover. This plant is easy and forgiving in less-than-ideal positions and would put up with the shade cast by big trees in summer.

So it is perfectly possible to conjure something from nothing in the short, dark days at the nadir of the year, but winter also gives gardeners time to look forward to and dream about spring. In the garden, spring means bulbs, as many as you can possibly pack in. This is the explosion we wait for with an impatience that is not equalled by any other event in the garden.

The Season for Bulbs

The best thing about bulbs is that you often forget you have planted them. Unlike many garden plants, they keep themselves neatly out of view for most of the time they are not performing. Then suddenly, in spring, there they are, not the slightest bit put out that you have not been worrying over them or making them special snacks. There is a dark side to this, of course. There always is. It is the mortifying experience of spearing a dormant bulb through the heart on the end of your garden fork. 'I'm so sorry', you say, and you rebury the stricken bulb with some special compost to soothe the wound. Bulbs have enough natural enemies to deal with (mice, birds, slugs, deer...) without their friends turning on them with unkind thrusts.

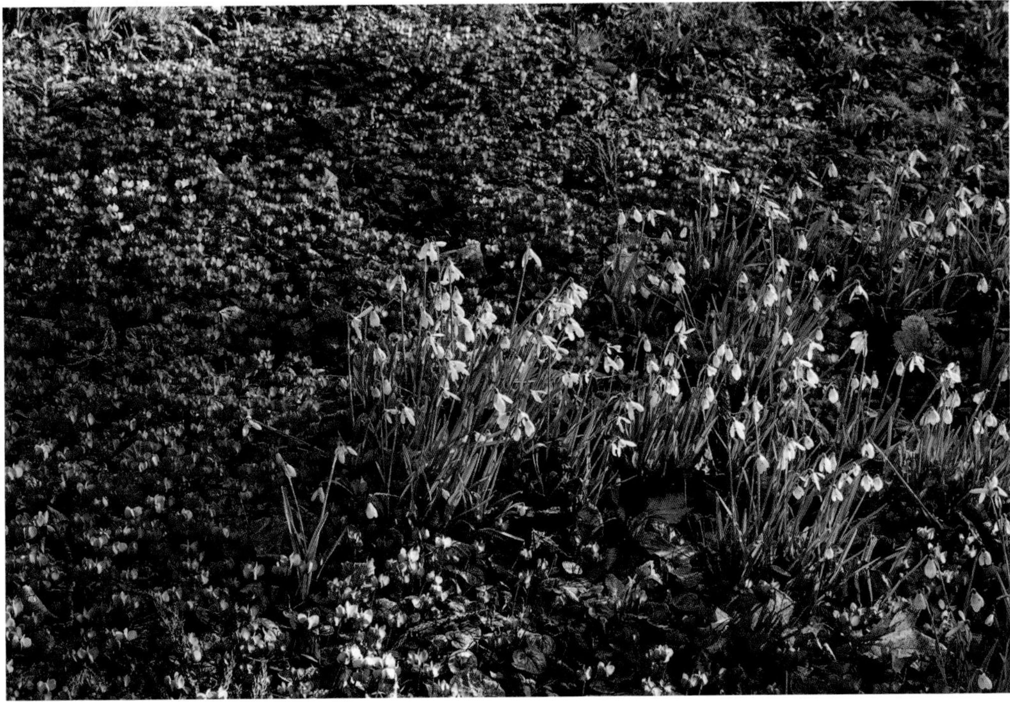

Top: The pale, speckled flowers of *Helleborus × hybridus* make strong clumps between a scattering of winter aconites (*Eranthis hyemalis*). Pushing through the blanket of winter leaves are snowdrops (*Galanthus elwesii* var. *monostictus*) and the seemingly fragile goblets of *Crocus tommasinianus*.

Above: Given space, as they have here in the garden at Colesbourne in Gloucestershire, UK, spring-flowering *Cyclamen coum* will seed itself about liberally. Here, the cyclamen is partnered with snowdrops.

The low light of an early spring evening illuminates one of the meadows at Great Dixter in Sussex, UK, home of the great plantsman, the late Christopher Lloyd. An early pioneer of meadow gardening, he persuaded both crocuses and light-limbed daffodils to naturalize in the turf. Over the years, both have spread liberally, creating spring scenes of breathtaking beauty.

Crocuses, massed in variety, are one of the most heart-lifting pleasures of an early spring garden. The only problem is that you have to double up like a croquet hoop to admire their finer points, the flush of bronze on the back of the enchanting *C. chrysanthus* 'Zwanenburg Bronze', the brilliance of the orange anthers inside 'Snow Bunting's virginal flower. You also need to choose your moment to admire them. Without sun they remain resolutely closed, while the cold dampness of winter soil gradually penetrates the soles of your boots.

Of course, there are mice to be dealt with, for they adore crocuses almost as much as gardeners do. The problem was noted almost as soon as crocuses began to be cultivated. An engraving in the *Hortus Floridus*, a nurseryman's catalogue of 1614, shows a mouse nibbling a crocus corm with all the devoted attention of a satisfied gourmet. E. A. Bowles, the famous Edwardian gardener who wrote a classic trio of books, starting with *My Garden in Spring* (1914), was a crocus fiend and consequently a psychopath where mice were concerned. 'Mice need fighting in all months and by any means', he wrote, and went on to recommend a complicated armoury of cats, poison, slippery jars sunk into the ground, and traps baited with brazil nuts. He had some no-nonsense ways with caterpillars as well.

But this was a man who was prepared to wait patiently for thirty years before his cross-fertilization programme produced a pure white seedling of the Greek species, *Crocus sieberi*. Such dedication excuses a certain paranoia. Bowles's delight was the species crocus, smaller but earlier flowering than the large varieties, now generally known as Dutch crocuses. Both types have their uses, but it is better to plant them in separate places. A bantamweight such as *C. chrysanthus* will be knocked sideways by a heavyweight Dutch crocus such as the grey-blue *C.* 'Vanguard'.

Since they like the same open, well-drained conditions, crocuses fit well with alpine plants such as saxifrages in a scree or rockery, and their Lilliputian scale works in that position. Some of the more vigorous *C. chrysanthus* types will cope in reasonably fine turf, along with early-flowering aconites and colchicums to fill the space in autumn. *C. tommasinianus* also grows in grass, provided it is not too rough. The species is a pale lilac colour, which darkens in the selected form 'Ruby Giant'. In the wild, this crocus grows in light woodland in former Yugoslavia, so it will put up with some shade. Interplant it with the delicate wood anemone and corms of spring-flowering *Cyclamen coum* (p.24). If you want the crocuses to increase by seeding, as they can, do not mow for at least two weeks after all the foliage has disappeared. The crocus's seed capsule sits almost on the ground and takes some time to ripen and shed its seed.

Choosing varieties is not difficult, once you have decided whether it is blue, white or yellow that you are after. The large-flowered Dutch varieties are the showiest. But remember that birds tend to attack yellow crocuses more often than white or blue. *C.* 'Jeanne d'Arc' is the best of the big whites, an elegantly shaped flower with brilliant orange stigmas. 'Pickwick' has large flowers of silvery lilac, feathered with purple. The biggest selection is among the purples – no crocus is truly blue. *C.* 'Remembrance', nearly always described as a rich blue, is actually mauve. But it is still an outstanding crocus, as is the deep purple 'Victor Hugo' and the paler 'Grand Maître', a refined lavender. Among the early species, varieties of *C. chrysanthus* and *C. tommasinianus,* you get more complicated combinations of colour. A clutch of them, such as *C.* 'Ladykiller' have handsome, deep purple petals edged with white. The insides of the flowers are surprisingly pure, the slightly bluish-white of skimmed milk. There are also some superb varieties streaked with bronze, a combination that does not yet exist among the big crocuses. *C.* 'Orange Monarch' bursts through the soil in a subtle livery of dark brown on a bright yellow ground.

One of the earliest of the narcissus to bloom, in a tribe that can show flowers for almost three months, is *Narcissus* 'February Gold', an appealing cyclamineus type of daffodil that has petals swept back like the ears of a piglet fronting a storm. It rarely hits the date its name suggests, usually bobbing up unabashed a month later, like a guest turning up for dinner on the wrong night. *N.* 'Jack Snipe' flowers at much the same time but is slightly shorter, with a golden yellow cup flaring out from a surrounding frill of white petals. Try it with golden-leaved feverfew (*Tanacetum parthenium* 'Aureum'; p.34). *N.* 'Jenny' is a much paler flower, the petals white, the trumpet a pale primrose yellow. It is a good variety for naturalizing in grass.

Like crocuses, daffodils generally flower best in full sun, though some species such as the Tenby daffodil (*Narcissus obvallaris*) and the wild Lent lily (*N. pseudonarcissus*) grow reasonably well in dappled shade. Narcissi such as the creamy-buff 'Cheerfulness' need a good baking during the summer to instigate flower buds the following spring. This applies to all the tazettas, as this type of narcissus is called. *N.* 'Minnow' is from the Mediterranean and used to sunbathing during the summer. It is only about 18 cm (7 in) high and produces up to four flowers on a single stem; the colour is soft yellow, the trumpet slightly darker than the surround. Both 'Minnow' and 'Cheerfulness' need well-drained soil. If yours is heavy, dig in some grit before you plant and set the bulbs on sharp sand in the planting hole. Bonemeal helps too, providing nutrients to help develop roots and flowers. *N.* 'Cragford', 'Geranium' and 'Scarlet Gem' are all equally prone to death by damp. Try them among the emerging foliage of herbaceous geraniums such as *G. himalayense* 'Gravetye'.

For their smell, you need the old-fashioned pheasant's eye narcissus (*N. poeticus* var. *recurvus*). The flowers are elegant and papery, with tiny, snub-nosed centres, deep yellow ringed with red. Pheasant's eye is a well-proportioned flower and looks good growing in wild areas of the garden. Although its overall style is exactly right for natural situations, it is late – which, if you are planting in grass, can be a disadvantage. When you are choosing bulbs for naturalizing, avoid overbred monsters. They will look as out of place as Madonna at a school coffee morning.

Bulbs that grow in shade are particularly useful, though there are not enough of them. The Spanish bluebell (*Hyacinthoides hispanica*) is excellent under trees and among the greenery of shade-loving ferns. The flower stem does not droop to one side like the English bluebell (*Hyacinthoides non-scripta*) but stands upright, with the flowers ranged all round it like a rather sparse hyacinth. The white variety is the best, very pure and icy, especially among the newly emerging fronds of shuttlecock ferns or contrasted with the dark, leathery foliage of *Euphorbia amygdaloides* var. *robbiae* (see p.34). It seeds itself, but not in such a determined manner as the English bluebell, which is a bully in the garden. As well as the white, it comes in various shades of blue – one mid-blue, one dark – and a washed-out pink, which is the least successful colour. The blues are excellent in mixed plantings with late narcissi such as pheasant's eye.

Most scillas naturalize easily and are charming components in any spring grouping. *Scilla bifolia* (see p.18) has purple-blue flowers, *S. siberica* (see p.30) is a slightly later variety with sky-blue flowers. *S.* 'Spring Beauty' is taller at 15 cm (6 in) and has flowers of a searing bright blue. All are lovely. They are easy to establish and better garden guests than grape hyacinths (*Muscari*), which always seem to have too high a proportion of leaf to flower.

All the smaller bulbs – anemone, chionodoxa, crocus, puschkinia and scilla – need planting in sizeable numbers. Use twenty of one kind rather than four or five different kinds. Chionodoxa is closely related to the scilla, but the stamens of chionodoxa are all held together, whereas those of scilla fan out separately. In the garden, they like the same conditions and are equally good in half shade. Try them between early hellebores. *Chionodoxa sardensis* is pale blue with a white eye, but the blue is not quite as good as the scilla's. You might say the same about *Puschkinia scilloides* var. *libanotica*, which has pale blue flowers held round the stem like a small hyacinth. The intense blue of the scilla is hard to beat. Try scattering them round clumps of herbaceous geraniums, where they will hold the space until the geraniums leaf up properly.

Hyacinths, daffodils, tulips and scillas all flower best when they have been well-baked the previous summer, but in a temperate climate the baking does not come often enough to realize most bulbs' full potential. Some bulbs – *Tulipa undulatifolia* for instance – are so gorgeous that you do not want to risk being without them, and so to cover all eventualities, you plant fresh each autumn. *T. undulatifolia* has brilliant crimson-scarlet flowers, the petals nipping in slightly at the waist and finishing in needle-sharp points. The backs of the outer petals are washed in a greeny-buff shade, so in bud it looks very sober. Then it flings open its petals and reveals itself as the wildly sexy flower it is, set off against leaves that are an elegant greyish-green. Try it among clumps of columbines. They will not be in flower at the same time, but the foliage is good on its own at this time of the year, greyish like the tulip's and finely cut.

Primroses and Other Pleasures

Some wise gardener once said that the secret of successful gardening was to find out what likes you and then to grow a lot of it. So if you have damp, heavy soil, grow plenty of winter- and early spring-flowering primroses. They are useful for filling ground that will be shaded later in the year, for they do not mind shade once they have finished flowering. If you have ordinary primroses in the garden alongside named varieties, you will find all kinds of muddy crosses appearing, for primroses are opportunistic breeders. Of the special kinds, *Primula* 'Sue Jervis' is a double – a pale peachy pink that looks good with the clear blue of a pulmonaria or with a variegated brunnera. *Primula* 'Corporal Baxter' is a deep red double, very luscious and robust. Try it with the wine-tinted foliage of *Helleborus × sternii*. *Primula* 'Miss Indigo' is a startling double blue, with a fine silvery lacing round the edges of the petals.

Do not waste double primroses on dry, thin ground. Dig in plenty of compost wherever they are to grow or, even better, manure. Like other classic cottage garden plants, they need an old-fashioned chamber pot culture. Grow them where they will be shaded in summer, but not where they will dry out. The plants clump up meatily where they are happy. In order to keep them flowering well, split them every other year after they have finished flowering. The simplest way to do this is to ease out the whole clump and pull it apart with your hands. It is quite easy to see where the breaks should come, for the plant arranges itself in a series of crowns, each of which will make a new plant. When you replant, add some bonemeal to the soil and do not let it dry out.

Wandering round the garden in late spring is like being at a party where people you have not seen for ages suddenly loom into view. You can put a name to them but you've forgotten exactly what they look like and how they talk. Meeting them again gives you a pleasurable sense of rediscovery. You remember why you liked their company – or not. The equivalent of the ubiquitous party bore are weeds such as ground elder, already pushing in around juicy peonies or leering at verbenas close by.

Many plant groups that give pleasure at this time of year depend on the borrowed foliage of other plants that have yet to flower or, in the case of *Cyclamen hederifolium* (see p.174), already have flowered. These are natural companions for spring-flowering scillas. Without the cyclamens' intricately veined leaves around them, scillas are much less interesting. Bulbs rarely have good foliage and benefit enormously from borrowed leaves. Try scattering *Scilla bithynica* among the lush, shiny leaves of *Arum creticum*.

You can also use the bronze foliage of early peonies such as *Paeonia cambessedesii* as a backdrop. The leaves of this peony are much finer than those of the usual kind of garden peony, most of which have been bred from *P. lactiflora*. *Paeonia cambessedesii* leaves are more pointed, glossier and finished on the undersides with a sumptuous red. The flower – mid- to deep pink – is not as showy as those of the garden hybrids, but it is worth waiting for.

Spurges (euphorbias) provide good backgrounds for bulbs too, for the sulphurous greeny-yellow flowers work well with a surprisingly wide range of other colours. Both pink and red tulips look gorgeous in front of a giant spurge such as *Euphorbia characias*. Look for *Tulipa* 'Ridgedale', a double late tulip of deep crimson overlaid with copper, or *T.* 'Amber Glow', a Triumph tulip of rich crimson with a gold base. The Triumph tulip 'Prinses Irene' (see p.36) is the right colour to set against spurges as well, either bright *Euphorbia epithymoides* (see p.36) or the duskier, bronze-leaved *E. × martinii*.

If the arms of *Helleborus argutifolius* (see p.32) were keener on staying upright, it would make a good background for tulips too. The foliage is handsome, and the ghostly, pale green flower heads are unselfish enough to play a supporting role behind more flamboyant flowers; but the mature stems have a tendency to crash suddenly to the ground as the new growth erupts from the centre. *Anemone blanda* can cope with the situation, though. When crashed upon, it philosophically pushes out flowers either side of the obstruction, unfazed and unfussy.

The foliage of groundcovering geraniums has not developed enough by this time of year to be of much help as a supporting plant, but thalictrum (meadow rue) is already good by now and has the same greyish tones as aquilegia leaves. You could set pale greyish-pink primroses among the thalictrum. If that is too 'twinset and pearls' for your taste, add a few clumps of a much darker red-purple primrose. It is like putting on a brilliant slash of scarlet lipstick to wake up a sleepy set of clothes.

Groundcovering bugle (*Ajuga*) will not flower until early summer, but the dark, glossy bronze foliage of the variety 'Atropurpurea' will usefully set off the blue flowers of some dwarf iris, such as *I. reticulata* 'Joyce'. But do watch it: having lulled you into thinking it is a Good Thing, it will then try to strangle the iris. A little bugle goes a long way. While the thin, grassy iris foliage remains above ground, staking a claim to its own *Lebensraum*, you may remember to keep the bugle clear of it, but once the iris foliage sinks under the surface of the soil, the bugle will smother it in an instant.

Pulmonarias are excellent foliage plants, but at this moment they are concentrating on flowering. The best leaves come later, when the flowers have finished. In this respect, pale blue *Pulmonaria saccharata* 'Fruhlingshimmel' does not earn its keep half so well as the much more richly coloured *P.* 'Lewis Palmer'. Besides being a better colour, the latter has more vigorous, upright growth. It goes well with the leathery leaves of Mrs Robb's bonnet (*Euphorbia amygdaloides* var. *robbiae*; see p.34). Both grow well in shade, provided it is not too dry.

Forget-me-nots will be starting to flower too, and there are some excellent seed strains with deep blue flowers; some have a tiny white eye. Try them mixed with a dwarf narcissus such as *N.* 'Rip van Winkle'. This does without trumpets entirely and produces instead a wild double head of two-tone yellow, more like a dandelion with attitude than a daffodil. It is mad but does not realize it.

Also mad, but elegantly so, is the two-tone grape hyacinth (*Muscari latifolium*). Instead of the grassy foliage that accompanies the normal grape hyacinths, this emerges with a single broad leaf wrapped around a navy-blue flower, finished off unexpectedly with a pale blue topknot. It makes a good companion for the buff double primrose 'Sue Jervis' and *Helleborus* × *sternii*, which has marbled foliage, purple stems, greeny-pink flowers and far too much disfiguring leaf spot. Cut them off as soon as you can.

Burgeoning Leaves

Although there is a tumult of flowers in mid-spring – primroses of all kinds, scillas, narcissi, pulmonarias, grape hyacinths, blue-and-white striped 'Columbine' violas, spurges – it is the great swelling mounds of foliage in the garden that make the whole place look rich and furnished again. Particularly vivid and brilliant at this time is the fountain of growth that comes from the giant fennel (*Ferula communis*; see p.168), a different group of plants from the fennel you eat but with the same fine, threadlike foliage. In good soil, this plant will make a fabulous mound of lacy green a metre (3 ft) or more across, and perhaps 60 cm (24 in) high. Then when it feels it has built up enough of a foundation, it sends up a huge flowering stem topped by flat heads of yellow flowers. The leaves are its chief glory, though 'leaf' sounds too meaty too hunky a term for this filigree-spun wirework. Combine it with the rapier leaves of a tall iris such as *I. orientalis* (see p.90) and a mound of brunnera, covered now with forget-me-not flowers.

Iris leaves – that is, the tall, spearlike kind that go with beardless irises such as *I. orientalis* and *I. sibirica* – are very useful at this time of year, acting like exclamation marks among low mounds of geranium leaves or thalictrum. You cannot use bearded iris in this way, for they resent having their rhizomes covered or shaded by vigorous neighbours. But *Iris orientalis* seems to grow anywhere, in sun or shade, the leaves eventually reaching a metre (3 ft) in height. The sword leaves of *Crocosmia* 'Hellfire' (see p.124) are equally obliging, spearing through low mats of early spring flowers such as the celandine *Ficaria verna* 'Brazen Hussy' or *Anemone blanda*.

The giant cow parsley (*Selinum wallichianum*; see p.76) is not such a hypnotically vivid green as the giant fennel, nor as finely cut in its foliage, but the heroic Edwardian gardener E. A. Bowles called it 'the queen of the umbellifers', and he did not hand out praise lightly. Planted out as a seedling, it seems improbable that it will eventually top 1.5 m (5 ft). Height is a difficult thing to bear in mind when you are placing plants. It is easier to feel their width, to be aware of sideways growth.

The selinum flowers with typical flat umbellifer heads in white, rather than yellow, but as with the giant fennel, its leaves are as important as its flowers. Sweet Cicely (*Myrrhis odorata*) is one of the few of the fern-leaved umbellifers to get its act together this early in the year. The foliage is a wonderfully fresh green, and by late spring it will already be in full flower with heads of greenish, greyish-white – not showy, but quite sweet smelling. The 'odorata' tag applies equally to flowers and leaves: they smell of aniseed. Sweet Cicely will grow in deep shade, where you might partner it with the spotted leaves of pulmonaria and the shiny strap foliage of hart's tongue ferns (*Asplenium scolopendrium*; see p.20). John Gerard (*c.*1545–1612), one of the early herbalists, said that to eat sweet Cicely was 'exceeding good, holsome and pleasant among other sallade herbes', but perhaps people then were keener on the taste of aniseed. In country areas, the plant was once used as a polish, rubbed into oak panelling and buffed to a shine when the juice had dried.

Sweet Cicely is a compact plant, no more than 60 cm (24 in) high and wide. You would not want it in a starring role, but it is useful because it is early and unfussy about shade. It makes a good backdrop for low mats of *Primula vulgaris* subsp. *sibthorpii*, which will be flowering now, each short-stemmed, pinkish-mauve flower displaying a yellow eye. This does not seed around like the common primrose, but the clumps are easy to split once flowering is over.

Variety in form is perhaps the first thing you notice in contrasts of foliage plants – upright iris sword leaves against chunky brunnera leaves, lacy sweet Cicely against the stout, spotty foliage of pulmonarias – but there are other contrasts to bear in mind too: contrasts of texture, colour, variegation, habit. The drooping quality of summer-flowering allium leaves, which initially grow up, then turn over on themselves so that their tips touch the ground, is a distinct landmark among the determinedly upright spears of peony foliage, pushing through the ground now with knobby flower buds firmly and bossily in place on top. Although you do not think of either alliums or peonies as being primarily foliage plants, they are both positive assets in mid-spring. Their real moment of glory will come later, when they flower, but how many plants is your garden carrying that contribute little outside their flowering period? Before you pick a new plant to fill a gap in your garden, ask it, 'What do you look like when you are not in your best clothes?' And be grateful that the plant cannot ask you the same question.

In her own spring border at Gresgarth Hall in Lancashire, UK, garden designer Arabella Lennox-Boyd has partnered *Pulmonaria officinalis* 'Sissinghurst White' with the neatly variegated leaves of *Hosta undulata* var. *albomarginata*. Echoing the pale tones of both foliage plants are the white blooms of *Narcissus* 'Ice Wings', with their long, elegant trumpets.

The arum lily is not evergreen, but it starts into growth at a time when most other herbaceous perennials have dived underground for the winter. Its growing cycle is a drama in three acts. First comes the superb foliage – the main reason to grow this beauty – each arrow-shaped leaf marbled with silver and edged with a narrow margin of plain green. In spring, the menacing spathe erupts, sheltering an unambivalent spadix. Finally, in a blood-red finale, a berried stalk takes the stage, by which time the leaves have quietly melted away. The astilbe, meanwhile, will have had its own peak, flowering in high summer, when the arum is between acts. The arum's finale is good, but its chief strength is its winter performance. At this stage, of course, the astilbe will have died down, leaving only dark brown flower spikes behind. Do not be in too much of a hurry to cut these down. They are wiry enough to stand upright in winter gales and look wonderful when glitteringly iced with frost. The scilla contributes only a short-lived shiver of blue, but it comes when we most want it.

Arum italicum 'Marmoratum' + *Astilbe* 'Irrlicht' (× *arendsii*) / *Scilla bifolia*

① *Arum italicum* 'Marmoratum'

HEIGHT: 15–25 cm (6–10 in)

SPREAD: 20–30 cm (8–12 in)

FLOWERING TIME: Mid-spring

STAR QUALITIES: Superb dark green, glossy foliage, elegantly veined in silvery white. The creamy white spathe is followed in summer by a spike of brilliant red berries.

ALTERNATIVES: *Arum creticum* has showier spathes but less arresting foliage.

② *Astilbe* 'Irrlicht' (× *arendsii*)

The foliage is deeply cut and ferny, providing a lacy underpinning for summer flowers that are borne in plumelike spikes, crammed with tiny florets packed together along the stems. This variety grows to about 60 cm (24 in). Although astilbes will thrive in sun or shade, they must have moist soil round their feet.

③ *Scilla bifolia*

Scillas will grow anywhere except in the driest and dustiest of soils; where happy, they will self-seed liberally. The starry flowers are a soft, purplish-blue, borne on stems rarely more than 15 cm (6 in) high. The leaves have the grace to allow the flowers to perform before they develop fully themselves. Plant bulbs about 7 cm (3 in) deep, and mulch them with leaf mould or sifted compost in autumn.

1

2

3

The hart's tongue is unusual among ferns, as the fronds are not divided, but boldly strap-shaped, with a rich, glossy finish. Consequently, a clump of these, though arching out in the symmetrical way typical of all ferns, is a meaty landmark in the garden. And it is evergreen, drawing more attention to itself in winter than it ever does in summer. Accentuate the drama of the new leaves uncurling by cutting away all the old foliage in early or mid-spring. This is a natural-looking, half-wild group of plants, useful for colonizing a shady area of the garden. They will be happy in quite dense shade, provided the soil is not starved or dry. Ferns are so sophisticated that they do without flowers altogether. They are nature's equivalent of the little black dress, accessorized here with lungwort (*Pulmonaria*) and honesty (*Lunaria*). In form, texture and colour, the lungwort's foliage contrasts strongly with the hart's tongue's leaves. Honesty provides extra stature and, with its seed heads, a ghostly winter backdrop for the fern.

Asplenium scolopendrium + *Lunaria annua* var. *albiflora* 'Alba Variegata' / *Pulmonaria officinalis* 'Sissinghurst White'

(1) *Asplenium scolopendrium* (Hart's tongue fern)

HEIGHT: 45–75 cm (18–30 in)

SPREAD: Up to 45 cm (18 in)

FLOWERING TIME: Evergreen fern

STAR QUALITIES: Year-round performance, with evergreen strap-shaped fronds, polished as highly as shoe leather. At its best in spring, when the new fronds uncurl, crozier-like, from the furred basal clump.

ALTERNATIVES: Capable, like other ferns, of producing many variations on the basic theme: the Crispum Group has strong, broad fronds, the edges crimped as though with curling tongs.

(2) *Lunaria annua* var. *albiflora* 'Alba Variegata' (Honesty)

The name is confusing, as this is a biennial. In the first year it makes a low plant, all leaf and lushness. The following year, it shoots up to flower 75 cm (30 in) high. The variegation on the leaves of 'Alba Variegata' lessens honesty's coarseness. Although good enough in flower (white in this variety), it is even more useful when the whole plant has been reduced to a bleached winter skeleton, hung with the flat silver discs of its seed heads.

(3) *Pulmonaria officinalis* 'Sissinghurst White' (Lungwort)

All the lungworts make excellent groundcover plants. They grow strongly, spreading to 60 cm (24 in), and when in full leaf between late spring and early winter, they smother annual weeds with ruthless ease. The best types, like 'Sissinghurst White', have foliage mottled and splashed with silver. The white flowers appear on 30 cm (12 in) stems in mid-spring, before the leaves are fully developed.

2

3

This group of plants will be happiest in damp woodland, a quite shady place where the corylopsis will get some shelter both from hot sun and early spring frost. Its soft primrose yellow flowers are charming, appearing in early spring before the shrub leafs up, hanging in graceful small bunches from the branches. Corylopsis gradually builds up into a dense, twiggy rounded mass, eventually reaching about 1.5 m (5 ft). It's a quiet, demure thing, but its flowers, as well as being early, are prolific and scented – a huge bonus. Partner it with companions such as trilliums, which will thrive in the same dappled shade and slightly acid soil. Trilliums have three wide 'leaves' that are actually bracts, supporting handsome, three-petalled flowers. The wake robin (*Trillium sessile*) has particularly eye-catching bracts, pale greeny-grey blotched with purple, with the narrow, deep maroon flower balancing on top. Use a plant such as epimedium to hold the ground after the corylopsis and trillium have finished their displays.

Corylopsis pauciflora + *Trillium sessile* / *Epimedium* 'Amber Queen'

① *Corylopsis pauciflora*

HEIGHT: 1.5 m (5 ft)

SPREAD: 2.5 m (8 ft)

FLOWERING TIME: Early to mid-spring

STAR QUALITIES: Very early into flower, and prolific. The pale primrose yellow blooms are scented and hang elegantly from twiggy branches.

ALTERNATIVES: *C. sinensis* var. *sinensis* makes a taller, wider shrub with longer 'catkins' than *C. pauciflora*.

② *Trillium sessile* (Wake robin)

The trilliums are a superb group of plants, with flowers that balance on the wide platform made by the showy bracts. Everything else is in threes too. Once the rhizomes have settled, you can expect to see the deep maroon flowers of *T. sessile* between early and late spring, providing a superb contrast with the pale corylopsis above them. In the wild, this species is a woodland plant, native to the eastern United States. When their act is over, they disappear completely.

③ *Epimedium* 'Amber Queen' (Barrenwort)

The epimediums are uncomplaining creatures, unfussy about soil and perfectly happy in shade. Leaves are topped in spring with long, arching spikes of flower, yellow in this selection, tipped with a warm orange-red. The spiny foliage is usefully semi-evergreen, best cut back in late winter just before the flower shoots come through the ground. A clump will spread slowly to 45–75 cm (18–30 in) across, with the flowers on strong, wiry stems reaching 15–25 cm (6–10 in).

1

2

3

Winter-flowering shrubs are particularly welcome in a garden, not only for their flowers but because so many of them – daphne, corylopsis, mahonia – are deliciously scented. In this respect, the daphnes excel. 'Jacqueline Postill', selected from a Himalayan species, starts flowering in the depths of winter, the small, waxy blooms, purple outside, white within, thickly spread among the sparser semi-evergreen leaves. *Cyclamen coum* flowers at the same time, in shades from deep magenta pink to pure white, while the maidenhair fern quietly froths between, happy in sun or shade. 'Jacqueline Postill' has a usefully narrow habit, so there is room, if you want, to add another smaller daphne, such as *D.* × *transatlantica* 'Eternal Fragrance', to extend the flowering (and the scent) of this patch further into the year. Daphnes are best planted small, so the roots are disturbed as little as possible. Once established, this relaxed trio will look after itself very well.

Daphne bholua 'Jacqueline Postill' + *Adiantum venustum* / *Cyclamen coum*

---

① *Daphne bholua* 'Jacqueline Postill'

HEIGHT: 3–4 m (10–13 ft)

SPREAD: 1.5 m (5 ft)

FLOWERING TIME: Mid-winter to early spring

STAR QUALITIES: Gorgeously scented, purplish-pink and white flowers, borne in great profusion. Graceful and narrow, the upright branches carry pale green, leathery leaves.

ALTERNATIVES: Evergreen *D. bholua* 'Darjeeling' flowers several weeks earlier than 'Jacqueline Postill' but in growth is not as robust. Other winter-flowering varieties include the European native, *D. mezereum*, with sweetly scented flowers in pink or white. The Chinese species, *D. odora*, includes a selection with variegated leaves, 'Aureomarginata'.

② *Adiantum venustum* (Himalayan maidenhair fern)

Ferns take their elegance and grace for granted. It is we crass humans who find them astounding, especially the lacy maidenhair family, with tiny slivers of green tremblingly attached to thin, wiry stems. Low-growing, no more than 15 cm (6 in) high, this fern puts up with a wide range of growing conditions. Shear off the old growth at the end of winter so you can marvel at the new bronze shoots that curl up from the basal clump.

③ *Cyclamen coum*

Enchanting snub-nosed flowers in white or various shades of pink. The best are a deep carmine. Rounded leaves, not as showy as those of *C. hederifolium* (see p.174), and variable in their patterning. The Pewter Group has leaves heavily overlaid with dull silver. Give this cyclamen plenty of room, for it is easily overwhelmed. The flowers, no more than 5–8 cm (2–3 in) high, appear between December and March; the wonderful foliage lasts longer.

2

3

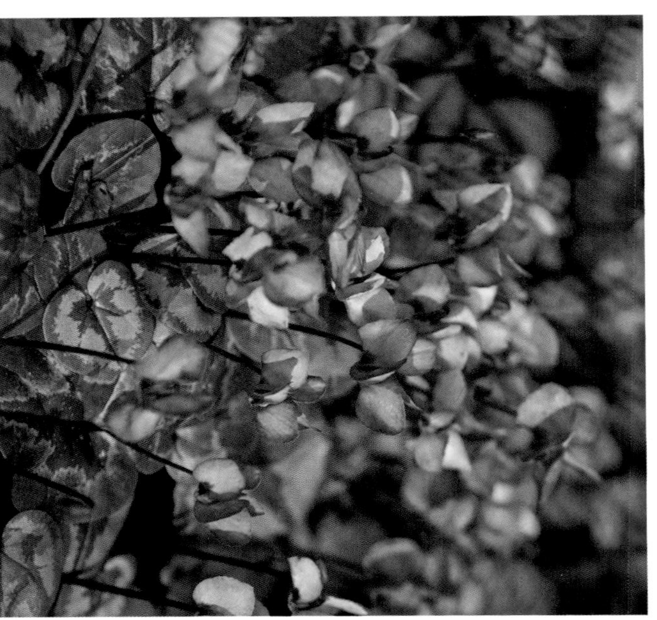

1

A damp, slightly shaded position will suit all these plants, none of which like to be baked or thirsty. The erythronium has star quality and will catch all eyes when it flowers, but like so many bulbs and corms, it has little to offer when its act is over. That is when you will be glad of the rhododendron, which grows quietly up and out to about 1.25–1.5 m (4–5 ft), just coming into leaf when the erythronium is flowering but producing its own white, beautifully scented blooms later, in mid-summer. The narrow foliage of the iris is through the ground by early winter, though the intriguing flowers will not show until late winter or early spring. This trio is well balanced in terms of stature and performance, giving a long season of interest. The iris hands on to the erythronium, but you still have the rhododendron to look forward to. Once planted, leave the erythroniums alone. They hate to be disturbed, though they will appreciate an annual mulch of leaf mould.

Erythronium 'Pagoda' + *Rhododendron viscosum* 'White Ness' / *Iris tuberosa*

① *Erythronium* 'Pagoda'

HEIGHT: 25–35 cm (10–14 in)

SPREAD: 15–20 cm (6–8 in)

FLOWERING TIME: Mid- to late spring

STAR QUALITIES: Gorgeous flowers of pale yellow. The petals bend back on themselves, revealing darker yellow stamens inside. The sparse leaves are glossy and faintly mottled.

ALTERNATIVES: 'White Beauty' has white flowers ringed with brown in the centre; *E. dens-canis* (dog's tooth violet) has pinkish-purple flowers above heavily mottled leaves.

② *Rhododendron viscosum* 'White Ness'

A selected variety of the North American swamp honeysuckle, which makes a fine display in early to mid-summer with its elegantly held white trumpet flowers. White stamens curl out on thin threads from the mouth of each one. It grows with a neat azalea habit, easy to accommodate in a limited space and deciduous, so the earlier flowers of the iris and the erythronium have the space they need to shine.

③ *Iris tuberosa* (formerly *Hermodactylus*) (Widow iris)

An astonishing flower, with petals of weird olive green and dark purple. The texture of the flower is like expensive satin, though no man-made material was ever produced in these subtle, bizarre colours. They are lovely to pick, to appreciate more easily the wonderful intricacy of the bloom, and they are scented. The leaves are thin and grassy and, by flowering time, much longer than the flower itself, which is generally about 27 cm (11 in) tall.

3

2

Spring should be Grand Slam time, and bulbs achieve those effects better than any other kind of plant. But while you are enjoying these in-your-face displays, you need always to be thinking, 'What happens afterwards?' You may feel that nothing will ever give you more of a lift than the spring-flowering tulip 'Little Beauty' interplanted with deep blue De Caen anemones. But something has to happen on that patch for the rest of the year, when both anemone and tulip have retreated underground.

If you add snaky, ground-hugging twirls of grey-leaved *Euphorbia myrsinites*, there will be a splendid sideshow to look at later. The euphorbia (spurge) flowers at the same time as the tulips and anemones, adding vivid lime-green heads to the mix, so the patch registers as a seasonal display rather than successional in its planting. But the euphorbia is a good all-round plant, evergreen (or rather, ever-grey), intriguing, sculptural. On its own, it will make this spot worth visiting long after the bulbs have gone.

Euphorbia myrsinites + *Tulipa* 'Little Beauty' / *Anemone coronaria* 'Jerusalem Blue'

(1) *Euphorbia myrsinites*
(Spurge)

HEIGHT: 5–8 cm (2–3 in)

SPREAD: 20 cm (8 in) or more

FLOWERING TIME: Early to mid-spring

STAR QUALITIES: Evergreen perennial, with whorls of small pointed leaves carried in spirals round the prostrate stems. Vivid heads of greenish-yellow flowers.

ALTERNATIVES: *Euphorbia cyparissias* has finer, fernier foliage on upright stems and is not evergreen; It flowers in late spring and is invasive, unlike *E. myrsinites*.

(2) *Tulipa*
'Little Beauty'

In flower by late March, this is a small (only 15 cm / 6 in high) but unmissable tulip. It has a flower of pure, unadulterated magenta, so brilliant that even the designer Schiaparelli would blink at it. The indeterminate white blotch at the base of the pointed petals is overlaid on the inside with a surprising rich blue. The same tenebrous blue-purple covers the stamens, which seem huge in relation to the size of the flower. If the sun shines, the tulips fling caution to the winds and open from globes into wide stars.

(3) *Anemone coronaria*
'Jerusalem Blue'

Anemone coronaria are the fat-stemmed, jewel-coloured anemones of florists' shops. The De Caen Group has single flowers, while the St Brigid Group has doubles. You can also choose separate colours such as the superb 'Jerusalem Blue', which is excellent for picking, as it has unusually long stems. 'Bordeaux' is a velvety purplish-red, equally gorgeous. Each tiny corm will provide as many as twenty flowers in succession, up to 25 cm (10 in) high – 30 cm (12 in) in the case of 'Jerusalem Blue'. Singles are more free-flowering than doubles.

3

2

1

The Lenten rose, *Helleborus × hybridus*, is a particularly useful plant because although not strictly evergreen, it never leaves a bare patch. The flower buds push through in mid-winter, and by the time they begin to fade, new leaves have grown up round them – lasting, glossily splendid, until the cycle begins all over again the following winter. Any kind of *H. × hybridus* is worth having, either the pale ones, with flowers freckled in green, or the deep purple, almost black ones, sinister enough for a witch's brew. The flowers droop on their stems like languid aristocrats. To admire the full complexity of the markings, you must go down on your knees, entirely appropriate in front of this plant. This hellebore is bewitching and mesmerizing enough to assume the key position in any plant group. Companions such as snowdrops and scillas will not get in the way of its extraordinary flowers. The chalk-white snowdrop will look most dramatic planted between almost black hellebores. Blue scillas will complement white or pale pink hellebores.

Helleborus × hybridus + *Scilla siberica* / *Galanthus elwesii*

(1) *Helleborus × hybridus* (Lenten rose)

HEIGHT: 45 cm (18 in)

SPREAD: 45 cm (18 in)

FLOWERING TIME: Late winter to early spring

STAR QUALITIES: Long-lasting flowers in a wide range of colours, from white to deepest slate purple, the pale ones often freckled and speckled inside with darker colours. Handsome, hand-shaped, evergreen leaves.

ALTERNATIVES: There are more than 250 different kinds of *H. × hybridus*, as well as other related hellebores such as 'Anna's Red', which has handsome marbled leaves. Buy seedling varieties in flower, when you can choose those with the best markings.

(2) *Scilla siberica* (Siberian squill)

This species has flowers that are usually later than *S. bifolia* (see p.18). The variety *S.* 'Spring Beauty' is a magnificent blue, growing 10–15 cm (4–6 in) tall. Plant the bulbs 5–8 cm (2–3 in) deep and about 8–10 cm (3–4 in) apart. Each autumn give them a top dressing of sifted leaf mould. Where happy, they will self-seed liberally.

(3) *Galanthus elwesii* (Snowdrop)

Eagerly watched for in the chilly days of mid-winter, the snowdrop is an accommodating flower. You can plant them as bulbs in late summer, but if you plant them 'in the green', with their leaves, just after they have flowered, they settle with little complaint. Single snowdrops, such as broad, grey-leaved *G. elwesii*, with pure white flowers swinging from elegant pedicels, are much prettier things than the bulbous doubles. The doubles look uncomfortable, their petals pulled in too tight at the top. You can almost hear them gasping.

1

2

3

This group has a strong winter presence, held together by the sculptural form of the mahonia. It is gaunt, but in a splendid way – stiffly upright, formal and evergreen, with leaflets arranged in pairs along a rib more than 30 cm (12 in) long. Spikes of yellow flowers that smell of cowslips burst in clumps from the growing tips of the upright branches. They start in early winter (November) and often last for several months. Mahonias flourish in sun or in quite deep shade and need little attention apart from a thick mulch each year. If the growths become taller than you want, shorten them in February. The hellebore has handsome, evergreen foliage, and its pale celadon-green flowers will begin just after the mahonia's have ended. After that, you still have the tall white flowers of the summer snowflake (*Leucojum aestivum*) to look forward to, filling any space between the hellebores.

Mahonia × *media* 'Lionel Fortescue'	+	*Helleborus argutifolius* / *Leucojum aestivum* 'Gravetye Giant'

① *Mahonia* × *media* 'Lionel Fortescue'

HEIGHT: Up to 5 m (16 ft) but can easily be kept shorter

SPREAD: Up to 4 m (13 ft) but can be reduced where necessary

FLOWERING TIME: Early to late winter

STAR QUALITIES: Provides a brilliant burst of colour when little else is in bloom; scented flowers; handsome, evergreen foliage on a shrub with a commanding presence. It is often badly used in so-called 'amenity planting'. Forget that, and give it the setting it deserves.

ALTERNATIVES: 'Lionel Fortescue' came from a cross made between *M. lomariifolia*, which has the best leaves of the tribe, and *M. japonica*, which has the best scent. 'Charity' and 'Buckland' come from the same cross and are almost as good.

② *Helleborus argutifolius*

This species has perhaps the most handsome foliage of all this extravagantly well-endowed group. The leaves are three-lobed, each of the stiff leaflets joined to the top of the stalk and edged all round with mock prickles. The green is matt and rather olive-coloured, a perfect foil for the great mounds of cup-shaped, pale celadon-green flowers that open in late winter. It grows equally happily in full sun or shade.

③ *Leucojum aestivum* 'Gravetye Giant' (Summer snowflake)

The snowflake has more by way of foliage than most bulbs. Already by early winter, this will be showing through, and the freshness of the leaf is a relief set in earth that has been scoured and beaten by the weather. The clumps of leaves are well established by the time the white flowers come in early to mid-spring. They look like overfed snowdrops, dangling from stems 50–100 cm (20–39 in) tall.

2

3

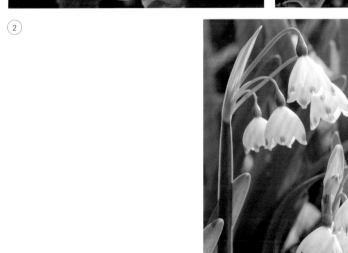

Make the most of *Narcissus* 'Quail's powerful spring scent, because when it has gone, there will be nothing else in this group to match it. Fortunately, it dies well; its leaves are dark and grassy, not in any way an eyesore in decay, like the leaves of monster-sized daffodils. There are two useful 'bankers' here to set off the lovely 'Quail' when it comes into flower and to hold the patch together when it has gone. The sober, dark spurge (euphorbia) is an excellent colonizer, though it has a mind of its own regarding where it puts itself. It thrives in a wide range of conditions, including deep shade, but appreciates a mulch of compost in spring. Cut out dead stems as necessary and keep an eye on its wandering feet. It is lovely with daffodils, which contrast both with the sombre foliage and the lime-green tones of the spurge's flowers. You will need to edit the group periodically, pulling up spurge where it is not wanted and transplanting or reducing new young seedlings of feverfew (*Tanacetum*).

Narcissus 'Quail' + *Euphorbia amygdaloides* var. *robbiae* / *Tanacetum parthenium* 'Aureum'

(1) *Narcissus* 'Quail'

HEIGHT: 35 cm (14 in)

SPREAD: 10–12 cm (4–5 in)

FLOWERING TIME: Mid- to late spring

STAR QUALITIES: A superb scent, like all the jonquils. There are several flowers to a stem, the petals and cups both the same rich, thickly textured golden yellow.

ALTERNATIVES: *N. jonquilla*, the species from which all the jonquils spring, is charming, and shorter than 'Quail'; *N.* 'Trevithian', another jonquil, has flowers of soft primrose.

(2) *Euphorbia amygdaloides* var. *robbiae* (Mrs Robb's bonnet)

This evergreen perennial spurge is an excellent colonizer for semi-wild areas in the garden, but is handsome enough to be used in a border as well. The leaves make dark, leathery rosettes, and in spring there are long-lasting heads of lime-green flowers. It grows about 30 cm (12 in) high and is a wanderer, spreading by underground stolons.

(3) *Tanacetum parthenium* 'Aureum' (Golden feverfew)

This is a short-lived perennial at best, never growing more than 30 cm (12 in) in any direction. It is an enthusiastic self-seeder, however, so the problem will be not in keeping it, but curbing it. On dull, foggy days in winter, young plants shine out like beacons, with low mounds of rich golden foliage. It is undemanding, which means that it is underrated. Its white daisy flowers that come in summer can be sheared off if they dissipate the look you are after.

1

3

2

The second half of spring should be awash with tulips. If you have heavy, sticky ground, the kind of situation that tulips hate, plant them in simple black plastic pots (big pots) and drop them into position behind mounds of spurge. The foliage of many plants – oriental poppies, fennel, geraniums, peonies – is tall enough to disguise the containers by the time tulips want to flower.

The particular limey yellow-green of this euphorbia looks wonderful with orange tulips such as 'Prinses Irene' (though it is far too subtle a tulip to be labelled as orange). Brilliant red tulips would be equally good, but yellow ones may get swallowed up in the colour of the spurge. Once this dazzling display is over, the geranium will get into gear and provide flowers all the way through until autumn.

Tulipa 'Prinses Irene' + *Geranium* 'Brookside' / *Euphorbia epithymoides* 'Major'

---

(1) *Tulipa* 'Prinses Irene'

HEIGHT: 30–35 cm (12–14 in)

SPREAD: 10–12 cm (4–5 in)

FLOWERING TIME: Mid-spring

STAR QUALITIES: Gorgeous markings of purple and hints of green streak the soft orange petals. A remarkable tulip with pale green stigma, yellow stamens and olive-green anthers.

ALTERNATIVES: *T.* 'Annie Schilder' has deeper orange flowers than 'Prinses Irene'; 'Orange Emperor' is earlier, with a green wash on the outside of the orange petals; 'Véronique Sanson' is a nicely proportioned flower and scented, an unusual bonus in a tulip.

(2) *Geranium* 'Brookside'

This is a vigorous, spreading plant with deeply dissected leaves that are covered with down when young, so that the foliage looks almost silvery. It flowers generously from mid-summer onwards, the rich blue petals of each bloom gathered round a small white eye. At 60 cm (24 in), it is taller than the similar *G.* Rozanne ('Gerwat') (see p.178). Like most herbaceous geraniums, it grows well in shade, provided it is not too dry. Shear down the plant in summer to get a second flush of flowers. 'Brookside' was found, as a seedling, at the University of Cambridge botanic garden and is named after the street that borders the garden.

(3) *Euphorbia epithymoides* 'Major'

This easy spurge makes a soft, rounded hummock of leaves about 50 cm (20 in) high and wide. It behaves like a true perennial, unlike its bigger cousin, the shrubby evergreen *E. characias*. The disadvantage of this is that it leaves a gap in winter, but it has wonderfully intense flowers that are an almost fluorescent greenish-yellow; they are not actually flowers at all, but bracts supporting insignificant flowers above. These last from mid- to late spring.

2

3

Erythroniums and trilliums are among the spring plants carpeting the ground under a fine magnolia in Keith Wiley's Wildside garden at Buckland Monachorum in Devon, UK.

II

Spring Turns to Summer

For a garden that is to satisfy you in the long term, you need to look further than flowers. Think of them as extras, the icing on the cake, and assess plants by other qualities instead. If it is a shrub, what is its overall shape? Does it have good fruits or seeds? Does it colour up in autumn? If it is a herbaceous plant, what sort of habit does it have? What are its leaves like? Are they well-shaped? Do they have texture? It is by manipulating all these attributes that you build up the best plant groups in a garden. Of course, flower colour has a part to play too, but it is by no means the most important consideration. Take epimediums: they are in flower at this time of the year, with white sprays on *E. grandiflorum* 'Nanum', crimson on *E.* × *rubrum* and clear yellow on *E. davidii*. The flowers are enchanting (though small), growing on strong, wiry stems well above the foliage. They are delicately made: four rounded inner petals curving down, four strappy outer ones making a ruff round them. But by the end of a month the flowers will be finished. What can the epimedium offer then to earn its place in the garden for the succeeding months? Plenty, for it has superb leaves that are held, often in arrangements of three, on thin, stiff stems. The leaf at the top of the stalk is symmetrically balanced, while the pair that face each other lower down are lopsided, the outer lobe of each pulled as if by gravity towards the ground.

The new leaves will be almost fully formed by the time the flowers finish, replacing the old foliage that has lasted through the winter. On *E.* × *rubrum*, the green is edged and smudged with mahogany. The shape and colour of the foliage, and the high gloss on the leaves of some varieties, make epimediums good mixers. They work well among clumps of cyclamen, another plant that has leaves at least as important as its flowers. They also sit comfortably between hellebores, particularly the hand-shaped leaves of *Helleborus* × *hybridus* (see p.30). But of course, to get these sumptuous effects, you have to provide the conditions that epimediums (and cyclamen and hellebores) enjoy: cool, moist soil with plenty of humus in it.

The Gentle Madness of Ferns

Ferns are confident enough to dispense with flowers altogether. Form is all, and undistracted by colour, you can settle to the engrossing business of finding them suitable partners. Set unfurling fronds of the common male fern, *Dryopteris filix-mas*, behind low spreading masses of silver-leaved lamium: uprights and horizontals. Use shuttlecock ferns (*Matteuccia struthiopteris*; see p.142) between clumps of the fat-leaved London pride (*Saxifraga* × *urbium*): lace and polished leather.

Ferns turn you into a collector because without any prompting, they try out such a huge variety of tricks. They suddenly produce flourishes like bunches of parsley at the ends of their leaves. They subdivide wildly to make leaf patterns more complex than the Amazon delta. A seemingly sensible, law-abiding fern such as the hart's tongue (*Asplenium scolopendrium*; see p.20) will suddenly flip its lid and perm the edges of its leaves into a series of frilly curves, or experiment with a black stem instead of a green one. Symmetry is built into them though, so even if a fern is acting like a lunatic, it is graceful with it. Grace is perhaps a fern's most important attribute, but it is a quiet one. Ferns do not tug at you as you walk by them. They just get on with being ferny and wait for you to notice them.

All ferns prefer some shade, but the golden-scaled male fern, *Dryopteris affinis,* and the soft shield fern, *Polystichum setiferum*, will put up with sun, especially if you can mulch to keep their roots cool. Try them with pink opium poppies or a tall yellow primula, such as *P. florindae* (see p.140). The big family of polypodys is equally obliging. The common polypody, *Polypodium vulgare*, will sow itself along the arms of old fruit trees or colonize the risers of a step. After a week or so with no rain, the fronds frizzle up completely, but then, like Japanese paper flowers dropped in water, they leap up again at the first wetting. Where polypodys colonize walls in the garden, they usually choose the north face.

To get the full drama of the ferns' uncurling, cut away the old dead fronds before the show starts. They all have slightly different ways of performing, but only the acrobatic shield ferns, the polystichums, have mastered the art of an effortless back flip.

The Iris Calendar

Sword-shaped leaves are great allies in mixed plantings, separating the rather sleepy, rounded clumps that so many herbaceous perennials grow into. You might, for instance, reach for the obliging *Iris orientalis* (see p.90). The flowers, white with yellow throats, appear in early summer, but by late spring the leaves will already be 90 cm (36 in) high, spearing through mounds of thalictrum, giving backbone to a rather spindly achillea, supporting a hummock of autumn-flowering sedum. This iris is a plant that, like the best sort of aunt, can get along in any company. The very similar Monspur Group irises, which belong to the Spuria Group, can be used in the same way. They make large clumps with the same strong, upright leaves as *I. orientalis*. The flowers are blue, shaped like the old fleur-de-lys. Use them with campanulas and lupins.

Where you want to create the same sort of effect on a smaller scale, use an iris such as *I. pallida* 'Variegata', which holds its leaves like bearded iris in flat, two-dimensional fans. They are broad, glaucous and, in this variety, striped with rich cream. The flowers are pale blue. They will provide a linking element between, say, the last stragglers in a patch of jonquils and the first flowering of a group of deep purple aquilegias. They also look lovely set in the midst of love-in-a-mist's ferny foliage.

All these irises sulk when they are moved; they need time to settle. The Spuria types are best planted in autumn, with the rhizomes set no more than 5 cm (2 in) deep in well-worked soil to which you have added some bonemeal. *I. pallida* needs more sun and can be planted in summer, with the top of the rhizome sitting above the ground, where it can get baked.

With some careful trawling among the catalogues, you can have iris in bloom for seven months of the year. Start with the little bulbous ones, such as *I. histrioides* 'Lady Beatrix Stanley' (see p.86) or *I. reticulata* types such as 'Blue Note' or velvety, purple 'Pauline'. These will see you through late winter and early spring. You also would not want to be without another winter-flowerer, forms of the Algerian iris, *I. unguicularis*, which thrive in poor soil at the base of a hot, sunny wall. *I. unguicularis* 'Marondera' has the biggest flowers of the group, in a clear mid-blue. 'Walter Butt' is much paler, the flowers rising from markedly upright clumps of leaves.

In mid-spring you should expect to see the first of the dwarf bearded irises, types bred from the European species *I. pumila*. Coast through late spring with different types of Dutch bulbous iris – the splendid 'Apollo' perhaps, with standards the colour of icebergs above falls of bright yellow, or 'Lion King', which is intriguingly marked in toffee-brown and purple. These are the irises that you see for sale in thin sheaves in florist shops, a promise of things to come when the weather outside is about as hideous as it can get. If you plant these bulbous irises in the garden in autumn, though, late spring is their most likely flowering time. They take up very little room and are extremely useful for slipping between clumps of herbaceous perennials such as geraniums, astrantias and campanulas, which at this stage are still not too leafy to overpower them. The iris foliage is thin and grassy, and when it has flowered the whole plant disappears underground, just like a daffodil.

Early summer is when the iris explodes. It is the season of the magnificent great bearded types, with poker-stiff stems and fans of grey foliage. The beardless *I. sibirica* also flowers now – not so showy, but a great deal easier to use in mixed plantings. There is also the delicious dwarf species *I. graminea*, with red-purple flowers smelling of ripe plums. This is ideal for patches at the front of a sunny border, as the grassy leaves are at most only 30 cm (12 in) high. Try it with the beautiful pasque flower (*Pulsatilla vulgaris*; see p.92) and aquilegias (columbine).

Iris flowers, models of symmetry, are built in threes: three outside petals, called falls, three upright petals, called standards, and right in the centre, three strappy petals called style arms, protecting the anthers. The beards of the bearded iris make hairy tufts down the centre of the falls. These are the showiest of all the irises but not the easiest to place in the garden. They need full sun for at least half the day and they do not like other plants flopping over their rhizomes. The lighter your soil, the easier you will find them. Alkaline soil is better than acid. Bearded irises range from dwarf – no more than 15 cm (6 in) high – to tall, which can be at least 1.2 m (4 ft). Modern breeding has brought about some spectacular flowers, frilled and ruffled, but it seems also to have made new bearded irises more susceptible to disease. Leaf spot is one of the worst. It usually appears just after flowering: small, round, brownish-grey spots that spread at an alarming rate. First the tips of the leaves wither, then the entire leaf collapses. Trim off the worst affected leaves. Avoid overhead watering and fertilizers high in nitrogen. Plant in places where plenty of air can run through the plants.

The French Impressionist painter Claude Monet adored irises, and in his famous garden at Giverny in northern France, tall bearded iris are set in strong, long lines down the edges of a sequence of narrow beds. These beds are heaped up into long mounds, like asparagus beds, and the garden itself is open and unshaded. This is what bearded irises like: good drainage at the roots and plenty of sun to ripen the rhizomes. For the authentic Giverny effect, use iris with lambs' ears (*Stachys byzantina*), forget-me-nots, purple tulips, mauve sweet rocket, tall alliums, dark purple wallflowers, aubrieta and opium poppies. Do remember, however, that the irises thrive at Giverny because they are planted on the edge of Monet's narrow beds, where the foliage of the other plants does not flop over them. They are not good sharers. If you plant them in mixed beds or borders, keep them, likewise, to the front, so that the rhizomes are open to light and sun.

Choosing plants to set together in the garden should be the most enjoyable part of making a garden. It is not a process that should keep you awake at night, worrying. If you choose plants carefully in the first place, combinations containing them will work more often than not. Some groups of plants, such as irises, violas, tulips, peonies and alliums, are breathtaking enough to transcend any surrounding disasters. You can enhance their beauty with thoughtful companion planting, but you cannot diminish it, however hard you try.

Friendly Faces

It is very much easier to love plants (and people) if they show some sign of loving you in return. To get violas on your side, give them damp, heavy ground. You may find that they grow better in half shade than they do in sun. All the violas have five petals, two making rounded ears at the top, two making cheeks at the sides and one pouting into a chin at the bottom, but the way that the petals are put together gives each variety a completely different character. Some are moon-faced, the petals running together into a gentle rounded shape, as with the superb *Viola cornuta* hybrid 'Eastgrove Blue Scented' or the lemon-yellow 'Judy Goring'.

Others have narrower petals that make long, rather peaky faces, as with the lovely 'Ardross Gem' (see p.94). This viola spreads out a low mat of foliage before raising its flowers well above the leaves on wiry 18-cm (7-in) stems. This gives an effect quite different to that of violas that like to have their leaves about them when they flower, pulling their foliage up around their necks like shawls. Try 'Ardross Gem' with a bushy thyme such as *Thymus* 'Porlock' and a dwarf pink geranium, perhaps *G. sanguineum* var. *striatum*. The viola will also grow well in a pot, though not as luxuriantly as it does in open ground. The mat of leaves spreads to cover the soil and stops it drying out, and the flowers bob about in the clear space above. Do not plant a viola in a pot smaller than 18 cm (7 in) – it will dry out too quickly. Nor should the pot be in full sun. They look very good next to monochrome potted succulents such as aeoniums and echeverias (see p.132).

The colours of violas are generally smudged, the blues always on the purplish side, the yellows often overlaid on the backs of the petals with purple, which sucks the intensity out of the primary colour. Few of the flowers are the same colour all over. Even *V.* 'Pasha', which seems to be a uniform dirty pink, has dark rayed whiskers leading to a tiny yellow eye. 'Pasha' is good with the foliage of a hellebore such as *Helleborus* × *sternii* 'Boughton Beauty'. Both enjoy the same kind of growing conditions, and both have been painted from the same palette, the weird pink of the viola appearing in a deeper shade on the stems of the hellebore. *V.* 'Vita' is similar, though a shade paler.

Violas are easy garden plants, because they are reasonably tolerant of a variety of growing conditions and make accommodating companions for plants that, as with the hellebores, have a completely different flowering season. They can, for instance, usefully disguise the collapsing foliage of colchicums, which are looking at their worst by late spring. But the colchicums' time will come just when you shear back the violas for their winter rest, and one show will drift seamlessly through to the next – or should. It is difficult to force yourself to chop the viola and waste its autumn flowers, but it is the only

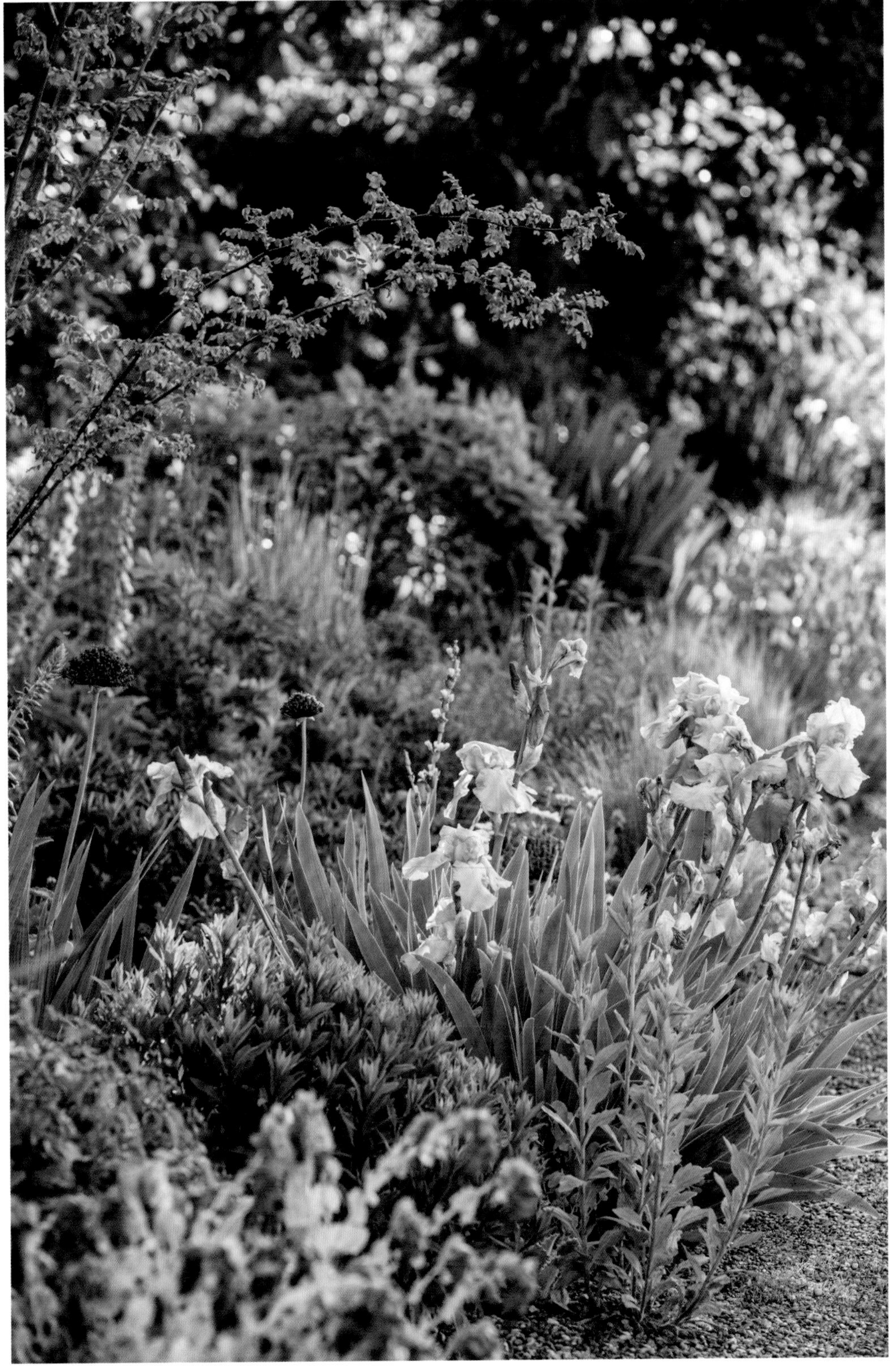

A glorious May border in the garden at Gravetye Manor in Sussex, UK, when the pale blue flowers of *Iris* 'Jane Phillips' are at their peak. Rising behind the irises are tall purple heads of *Allium atropurpureum* and *A. cristophii;* in the foreground the glaucous foliage of annual *Cerinthe major* echoes the grey tones of the iris leaves.

job violas require, apart from the deadheading that is vital to keep the plants on their feet.

The fact that you can never quite describe the exact colour of any particular viola is an advantage. Their smudgy colours, like chameleons' skins, adapt to whatever company they find themselves in. The silvery-mauve flowers of the old favourite *V.* 'Maggie Mott' look cool with grey artemisias but change their character completely when combined with the warmer shades of verbenas. The real Maggie Mott lived at a house called Scotswood in Sunningdale, Berkshire, southeast England, where her family had a gardener who was a viola fancier. He named a seedling after his employer's daughter and showed it at the Royal Horticultural Society in 1902. It appeared in the Society's viola trials in 1904 and has been in cultivation ever since. It flourished in India in the 1930s, when the garden designer John Codrington used it in the gardens of the Residency in Delhi. The Commander-in-Chief, Sir Philip Chetwode, had grandiose ideas for a large circular pool at the end of a vista there. The pool proved too expensive a project, so Codrington planted a huge circle of 'Maggie Mott' violas instead, their silvery colour giving the illusion from the Residency windows that there really was water at the end of the view.

The darkest of all the violas, and perhaps the blackest of all flowers, is *V.* 'Molly Sanderson', which has petals with the sheen of expensive satin. It is not as easy to place as other violas. Some time ago there was a vogue (fortunately brief) for all black gardens, where you could see 'Molly Sanderson' combined with grassy black ophiopogon and dark chocolate-scented cosmos. None gained in the association. Nor should you be tempted to use this dark, saturated shade with white-flowered plants, such as the low-growing *Achillea* × *huteri* – the contrast is too obvious. Try it instead with the misty blue of a veronica such as *V. prostrata* 'Spode Blue', or the magenta of a verbena.

When you are planting violas, think cool, think damp. They will not flourish in the dry shade under trees, nor will they be happy in light soil in full sun. Mulching around plants improves them wonderfully, for it retains moisture in the soil and keeps the roots cool. Liquid feeds help too, particularly in bolstering up plants after you have sheared them down in autumn. Unfortunately, slugs have a great fancy for violas – a fatal flaw in the so-called balance of nature. If slugs ate bindweed, it would be much easier to believe that we are, indeed, part of some Grand Design.

Of Tulips and Wallflowers

No garden can have too many tulips. This is one of the few infallible rules in gardening. There are thousands of varieties to choose from, but for some of the most interesting ones, look in the groups called Lily Flowered and Single Late (the Single Lates are sometimes labelled Cottage tulips). There is a lot of old blood coursing round in these groups, and the flowers sometimes do surprising things, throwing back to colours and forms that we never normally see. Try *Tulipa* 'Alabaster', a pure white flower that has been around since at least 1942. Nobody knows who raised it, which is always a good sign. It grows to about 60 cm (24 in) and flowers in late spring. Or maybe try gorgeous 'Greuze', first introduced to gardeners in 1891, a rich purple tulip that flowers in late April. Combine the beautifully formed blooms of Lily Flowered tulip 'White Triumphator' with yellow doronicum or a cloud of blue forget-me-nots. Set the incomparable Lily Flowered tulip 'Ballerina' – orange petals with a darker overlay – among smudgy clumps of *Euphorbia* × *martinii* (see p.84). Use richly coloured tulips such as luscious purple *T.* 'Jan Reus' or orange-brown 'Cairo' to give a spring lift to drifts of later-performing grasses, such as miscanthus and calamagrostis.

Get into the habit of having a backup supply of crowd-pulling tulips, which you can grow in plain black plastic pots and then drop into any bare bit of bed or border. By mid- to late spring, foliage is growing fast, so peony leaves, campanulas or fennel soon disguise the pots themselves. You might try, for instance, bringing in pots of the tulip 'Blue Parrot' to complement the restrained and handsome foliage of the hosta 'Krossa Regal' (see p.140). This has greyish leaves, but the stem grows unusually long before the elegant, not-too-broad leaf begins to develop. The plant stands high and urnlike.

Pots confer another advantage. If your ground is heavy, sticky clay (in a word, hideously unsuitable for bulbs), pots allow you to arrange drainage (critical for so many bulbs) more easily. Put 2–3 cm (1 in) of sharp grit at the bottom of the pot, then a layer of compost. For this, I make a mix of two scoops of a rich loam-based compost (John Innes No.3) with one scoop of 6 mm (¼ in) grit. Settle the bulbs comfortably into this bed, then cover them with more compost. It is much easier than trying to burrow holes into some clay maw, some vortex of stickiness which you know is going to be a coffin for bulbs designed for ground as fast draining as a sieve. A bulb planter, which works well when you are planting in grass, is not so useful in open ground, where the plug of earth that you draw out tends to crumble to bits.

Some pots are for display, but for settling into gaps, use simple, cheap, black plastic pots. It's not worth using anything smaller than 30–35 cm (12–14 in) across, because you cannot then stuff in enough bulbs to make a splash in a border. You can use your own home-made compost, unsieved, in the bottom half of the pot, where the bits of stick and stalk will help with the drainage, then put sieved compost on top of the bulbs. To discourage birds and slugs, finish off the pots with a top dressing of 6 mm (¼ in) grit.

If purple is the theme, tulips will give it to you in vast variety. *Tulipa* 'Negrita' is a star – a Triumph, or mid-season tulip, with a habit of throwing more than the usual six petals, so the flowers are astonishingly full and blowsy. It grows to about 45 cm (18 in) and flowers in late spring. It is lovely with forget-me-nots and cream-coloured wallflowers. 'Purple Prince' is another winner, slightly earlier and shorter than 'Negrita', but with the same rich, lustrous colour. 'Black Hero' is a stunning tulip, tall for a double and with a strong stem. It arose as a sport from 'Queen of Night' and is very much better.

Only occasionally does this wondrous family disappoint. *T.* 'La Belle Epoque' is formless and the colour of ancient corsets. Recent breeding of tulips has, it seems, been driven more by colour than form. *T.* 'Arabian Mystery', described as 'a wonderful rich violet-purple, silvery white at edge of petals' is a dog's breakfast. The silvery edging makes the flower look as though it is sick, or bleaching badly in the light. But there are few failures, and they are effortlessly eclipsed by marvels such as purple 'Bleu Amiable'. Use this with the Lily Flowered tulip 'China Pink' among forget-me-nots, variegated honesty and elegant *Gladiolus tristis*.

Of all the purple tulips, 'Blue Parrot' is the best – though not blue at all, of course, since that is one of the few colours that a tulip rarely produces. It is not even particularly parrotlike when compared, for instance, with the crazy 'Weber's Parrot'. Its petals curl in on themselves, making a somewhat congested flower. The colour is good: old-fashioned Victorian purple, which also runs down the top part of the flower stem. The leaves are narrowish and pointed, well-proportioned in relation to the flower. This is not always the case with tulips, some of which have foliage that is much too meaty. The base, hidden under the curling petals, is a surprising peacock blue. This is a handsome, elegant, classy tulip, which comes into flower in late spring. You may find that it zooms straight into the category of Tulips You Cannot Possibly Live Without. *T.* 'Brown Sugar' should be there too, a beautifully shaped flower with exceptionally pointed petals. The colour is a toffee-orange, very lovely. So should 'Havran', a tulip of superb form, with thick petals of lustrous maroon, velvet-textured on the outside, glossy within. And how can you continue happy without growing 'Exotic Emperor'? This is a superbly dramatic tulip, almost double, intriguing and handsome, the white flower clasped on the outside by strange green-striped claws, like the calyx of a rose. There is no other tulip like it.

Tulips are natural companions for wallflowers (*Erysimum*), and though wallflowers are often badly used, they are never hackneyed. Their rich tawny colours consort well with both tulips and daffodils, and the smell, when a warmish shaft of sun tickles their scent glands, is a glorious antidote to the sloth brought on by winter hibernation. A late spring garden should be swooning with more scents than a seraglio: one sniff of a wallflower can open up a whole Pandora's box of emotions: rows, reconciliations, a particular meal, a birthday party.

The precise smell of a wallflower is not easy to conjure up. Spicy, but which spice? It is odd that a smell so memorable when present should be so elusive when not. And we always think of wallflowers in terms of rent-a-crowd, never as a solo star. One wallflower is a ludicrous proposition. Daffodils, which suffer from the same difficulty, at least had a poem written about them. You have to use wallflowers en masse. They are not in themselves beautiful objects, though if you have room to allow them to become the perennials that they are by nature, rather than ripping them from the ground when they have finished flowering, they develop into venerable, sprawling plants, good when seen flopping over the edge of a raised terrace bed, or best of all, out of a crack in a stone wall. If badly grown, they are leggy, scraggy things, but they have the potential to be outstanding. There is that smell, and a wonderfully gloomy range of colours – rich mahogany as well as pale cream, dirty purple and glowing ruby. There is a mixture called *Erysimum cheiri* 'Persian Carpet' that exactly describes the effect wallflowers give. You can also get separate colours.

Tulips, including orange lily-flowered 'Ballerina' and purple 'Havran', explode from an underplanting of silvery *Brunnera macrophylla* 'Jack Frost' in June Blake's garden at Tinode, Co. Wicklow, Ireland.

If you are planting them with bulbs, plant wallflowers first, bulbs after, to avoid accidentally spearing bulbs hidden underground. If you are buying wallflower plants rather than growing your own, remember that what you buy in autumn is what you will see in spring. If you buy measly plants, they will still be measly, though in flower in spring: little extra growing takes place during winter. Look for plants that have rounded, well-developed heads of foliage rather than single stems, and get them into the ground as soon as you can. Height depends to a certain extent on variety. Standard wallflowers grow to about 45 cm (18 in), but there are various dwarf strains with names such as *Erysimum* 'Tom Thumb' that are considerably shorter and useful if you are trying to get the essence of the season in the space of a windowbox.

Along with stocks and sweet Williams, wallflowers are archetypal cottage garden plants. The bedding craze of the nineteenth century brought them into grander homes, but they have never been looked on as stylish plants. Today's plant snobs may spurn 'Persian Carpet' and its kind and instead search out plants of *E.* 'Bloody Warrior', with oxblood red double flowers set rather far apart on the stem. The special wallflowers 'Bloody Warrior', 'Harpur Crewe' (a double yellow), 'Baden Powell' (smaller, but otherwise much the same) and the wallflower-like *Erysimum* 'Bowles's Mauve' (blue-grey foliage and soft purple flowers) are later to come into flower than the common sorts grown from seed, which flower from mid-spring to early summer. The specials will not start until late spring. Wallflowers are sociable plants. Try *E.* 'Primrose Monarch' with pale blue pansies, or black violas if you are looking for a more dramatic contrast. For the authentic Monet effect, use clear yellow wallflowers with forget-me-nots. Enhance the rich mahogany shades with tulips such as brownish *Tulipa* 'Abu Hassan' or the elegant lily-flowered 'Pretty Woman'.

Celestial Peonies

Old-fashioned, late-flowering Cottage tulips also consort well with old-fashioned peonies – the deep crimson, double-flowered kind. The flowers are named after Paeon, physician to the Greek gods, because the old European variety, *Paeonia officinalis*, was looked on as an elixir for all ills. It was said to cure jaundice, kidney pains and epilepsy, to prevent nightmares and lift depression. It took off as a garden flower in the mid-nineteenth century, when the French nurserymen Jaques Calot, Auguste Dessert and Felix Crousse began some fancy cross-breeding, using *P. officinalis* and the Chinese species *P. lactiflora*. There are now at least 150 hybrids to choose from; a current favourite is an American hybrid called 'Buckeye Belle', a semi-double peony of zinging bright red. 'White Wings' is another fine peony, with single white flowers and foliage that colours well in autumn. Try it with a carpet of London pride in front, a cardoon behind and a sprawl of blue *Geranium × magnificum* beside it, or spikes of some piercing cobalt delphiniums. The common double crimson peony opens in late spring, most of the hybrids in early summer. Doubles last longer in flower than singles but are more difficult to stake and keep the right way up if there is a rainstorm. There is also a third type, which has strong, bowl-shaped outer petals like the singles, but with stamens that have turned into thread-like petals, making a huge fluffy boss in the centre of each flower. Sometimes these are the same colour as the outside petals, sometimes they contrast. 'Bowl of Beauty' is a good peony of this type, featuring rich pink petals with a creamy-white centre. Of the doubles there is no end, but some, such as pink and cream 'Madame Calot', are more sweetly scented than others. Henry Mitchell, gardening correspondent of the *Washington Post* until his death in 1993, described the doubles as 'dahlias that have gone to heaven'. Use them with brunnera and the brilliant spurge *Euphorbia epithymoides* to transform late spring borders.

As interest in the flower grew, more wild species were introduced into English gardens, including the impossibly named *Paeonia mlokosewitschii*. Most people just call it Molly the Witch. It has single pale lemon sherbet-coloured flowers over bronze-grey foliage. It is a beautiful species from the Caucasus, sometimes flowering as early as late April, a little earlier than *P. tenuifolia*, with fine, thread-like foliage and blood-red single flowers. In our garden it grows with witchy arisaemas and sheaves of leaves from false indigo (*Baptisia australis*), which flowers any time between April and June. My own favourites among the herbaceous peonies are those with good foliage, such as 'Early Windflower', a cross between two species that emerges early with superb, intricately dissected foliage of deep burnished bronze. It provides the best possible background to tulips before it even thinks of flowering itself. When it does produce its single white blooms with a central boss of gold, it is a show-stopper. A loud 'BOO' to those who say peonies are not worth planting because the flowers don't last long. Every garden should have at least one.

The herbaceous peonies die back completely during winter. Very different in habit are the so-called tree peonies, which are actually more like shrubs than trees. These slowly build up a permanent framework of gaunt, woody branches that add a wonderfully sculptural element to the garden in winter. Unbelievably vast flowers spring forth from these branches during May. These peonies, *P. × suffruticosa* and their kind, need more time to show you what they can do, but they are worth any amount of waiting. Plant them deeply, with the growing point about 10 cm (4 in) below the surface of the soil. Some tree peonies are grafted on to roots of herbaceous peony. Shallow planting in this case will encourage shoots from the rootstock, and those will not be the ones you have (expensively) paid for. Deep planting will encourage the grafted bit to make its own roots, which is what you want.

They are, anyway, slow growers. There is a well-known mantra among peony lovers: 'First year sleep, second year creep, third year leap.' You will have bought a stick in a pot and it will be some years before you see your tree peony build itself up to an open branched shrub, about 1 m (3 ft) tall. The foliage is outstanding, deeply cut and produced in a wide range of bronze-greens. As for the flowers, expect blooms up to 30 cm (12 in) across, madly ruffled, red, white, pink, yellow. I have white 'Renkaku' and dark maroon 'Kokuryu-nishiki', both of which have slowly built up to be superb plants. We inherited shrubby *P. delavayi* (see p.80), which grows up to 2 m (6 ft) tall but has small flowers, of a satiny, deep red. In season, it is one of the best things in the garden. Tree peonies will grow in semi-shade, but flowering is better if the wood is ripened by the sun.

If your tree peony starts sprouting the wrong kind of shoots, cut them off below ground level in late spring. You'll know them by the foliage, which is different from the foliage of the actual tree peony. The shrubs do not need regular pruning, but dead leaves tend to hang on through winter and are best removed in spring. Shorten any shoots that may have died by cutting back to a fat new bud.

The simple division between herbaceous peonies and shrubby ones was made more complicated in the late 1940s by the Japanese gardener Toichi Itoh, who crossed tree peonies with herbaceous kinds to produce the rather clumsily titled Intersectional Hybrids. These look more like herbaceous peonies than the tree ones, but they flower for longer, and you can get them in delicious shades of apricot and cream, which are colours the purely herbaceous kinds do not do. The Intersectional Hybrids are easy but, like the tree peonies, slower than herbaceous peonies to reach their full potential. The first one I grew was the exuberant lemon-yellow 'Bartzella', with huge, scented, very double flowers. I now have 'White Emperor', which produces white flowers streaked in purple, and 'Sonoma Velvet Ruby', a gorgeous deep, rich red. If these peonies could choose, they would opt for an open, sunny spot in rich soil, slightly on the heavy side. If you have light soil, mulching will help. They may need staking, which is most neatly done early in the season, using twiggy bits of hazel or birch, pushed in round the plant and roughly woven together over the top.

The Allium Brigade

Alliums, together with anemones, camassias, muscari and galtonia, all carry the bulb display from late spring into summer. The alliums are an enormous family, with more than 120 different types listed by specialist growers. They are found wild all over the northern hemisphere, in the Middle East, western China, around the Mediterranean and in the Pyrenees and the Alps. Most are hardy and easy to grow. The outline of the flower, usually a firm, round ball balanced on top of a sturdy stem, is strong and well defined – useful among the amorphous mounds and hummocks of herbaceous border plants. If you grow them among herbaceous plants, stick them well down in the earth, 12–15 cm (5–6 in) deep. This makes it less likely for the bulbs to be speared on your fork during the autumn clean-up, when you may well have forgotten their existence.

Some of the smaller alliums look particularly good in gravel and will give a good display for a month in early summer. *Allium cernuum* has wiry stems about 45 cm (18 in) long, topped with drooping clusters of small, beadlike pinkish-purple flowers, twenty or more

Top: The spurges (*Euphorbia* sp.) are invaluable garden plants and their arresting flower heads of piercing yellow make a memorable contribution to a late spring border. Here they accompany the dramatic heads of purple *Allium cristophii*.

Above: A private garden in Herefordshire, UK, where columbines (*Aquilegia vulgaris*) in several shades, from deepest purple to pale pink and blue, mingle in a happy, relaxed mix with *Tellima grandiflora* and *Anthriscus sylvestris* 'Ravenswing'.

in each head. It is an elegant plant, and there is not too much of the undistinguished foliage to detract from the main event. Try it with the small black-faced viola 'Molly Sanderson' and blue-grey lady's mantle (*Alchemilla erythropoda*). With these smaller alliums, you need correspondingly small companions. Try *A. azureum*, which has flower heads no bigger than a golf ball, on gravel or scree between low creeping mounds of thyme (*Thymus serpyllum*), with thrift or among grey-foliaged pinks.

Some alliums are as good in death as they are in life. This is especially true of *A. aflatuense*, *A. cristophii* and *A. schubertii* (see p.58), which die to become huge greenish or buff drumsticks on stiff stems. *Allium cristophii* has a stout stem only 60 cm (24 in) high and stands up well to bad weather. The biggest heads are 20–25 cm (8–10 in) across, perfectly round and made up of masses of starry, soft purple flowers. Each has six thin symmetrical petals, and the flowers cluster in a ball at the top of the stem, a firework frozen at the moment of explosion. Try *A. cristophii* with blue camassias among clumps of the airy grass *Calamagrostis × acutiflora* 'Karl Foerster' (see p.58), or with catmint and the tall white *Phlox carolina* 'Miss Lingard'. It also looks splendid rising from a hazy spread of sky-blue nigella, or jostling the rich blue flowers of *Geranium* 'Brookside' (see p.36). You could try one of the taller alliums interplanted with silybum (milk thistle), a plant like a variegated thistle that is rather better in youth than it is in old age. It is a biennial, dangerously domestic-looking in its first year, when it hugs the ground with crinkly foliage, the dark leaves splashed and veined with silver. In the second year comes an immense flowering stem, then death. Time to try a different combination.

Is Variegation a Good Thing?

A variegated plant will not necessarily be a better choice than the plain-leaved alternative. While it is true of silybum, which is only worth growing for its silver-splashed leaves that look wonderful interspersed with the feathery foliage of young fennel plants, too many variegated plants in the garden can look like a bad outbreak of spotty rash. And some variegated plants just look sickly, gasping for a good dose of chlorophyll. But carefully used, variegated plants can be winners. First, as always, you should think about what the plant needs in order to grow successfully. Some need to be in shade if the leaves are to stay strongly marked, while others will do best in full sun. Second, bear in mind that in any mixed group, a variegated plant will be the one that draws the eye. It will do best in an unfussy setting, with plants that are strong enough not to be browbeaten by their showier neighbour.

Resist the temptation to plant several different variegated plants close together. Instead of standing peacefully by one variegated treasure, quietly absorbing its pleasures, you will find that your attention is leaping like a frog from what is in front of you to the next variegated clump. The smaller the garden, the more restrained you need to be. The variegated comfrey *Symphytum × uplandicum* 'Variegatum' is a coarse, brash, showy plant that always attracts attention, with great hairy leaves in two shades of grey-green, each with a wide margin of creamy-white. The leaves emerge in mid-spring, and in late spring the plant throws up flower spikes of a bluish-mauve that will look good until early summer. When the leaves start to become dog-eared, you must shear the whole plant down to the ground. It will then throw up a second crop of good leaves, which have a much longer season than the first.

But this splendid bully will completely terrorize feathery companions such as astilbe or achillea. If you think the comfrey's bold leaf will be a good anchor for them, you are wrong; it will drown them. Try it instead in front of a stand of angelica, which will give it a cool, architectural setting. The commanding angelica will not be cowed by the comfrey's power play.

In pulmonarias, variegation is a must. The plain-leaved ones contribute far less after the spring flowering period. Where you might want a plain green and blue effect, rather than using *Pulmonaria angustifolia* 'Munstead Blue', try omphalodes, which flowers much more freely and brightly. The variegated *Pulmonaria saccharata* is particularly pleasant, with pointed leaves splashed rather than spotted with silver. The flower spikes come through in early to mid-spring, with blooms that drift between pink and blue. Then there is a hearty crop of leaves, very useful under some fairly plain, tall planting – ferns, perhaps, or giant fennel. The Argentea Group has leaves that are almost completely silver. In a planting of pale shades, *P. officinalis* 'Sissinghurst White' (see p.20) would be the one to go for.

Astrantia is always a good-tempered plant, variegated or not, with flowers that have the curious papery texture of everlastings. *Astrantia major* 'Sunningdale Variegated' is particularly choice, its leaves splashed boldly with cream. It is not fussy about soil but may lose its variegated markings if planted in full sun. It looks good alongside plain blue-flowered brunnera, or next to the purple-flushed leaves of the herbaceous clematis *C. recta* 'Purpurea'. A dark-leaved bugle such as *Ajuga reptans* 'Atropurpurea' running around its base also suits it. Use the astrantia as an underplanting for some sober shrub such as arbutus or a purple-leaved elder. This is one of the most rewarding ways to use variegated plants, by making them the lowest layer of a three-tiered planting: ground-hugging plants, shrubs, then a light-limbed tree shading its friends below. Small variegated periwinkles, such as the various forms of *Vinca minor,* look enchanting snuffling around under taller stands of hydrangea or corylopsis. Periwinkle flowers can be single or double, in blue, purple or white. Spotty pulmonarias can do the same kind of thing, but more hairily and thuggishly.

Some plants, such as hostas, have easy-going genes that can be encouraged to produce variegated foliage of astonishing variety. The background colour may be bluish or yellowish, the contrasting markings lightly or heavily applied. If you want a cool planting scheme, look for hostas variegated in white. Yellow-variegated hostas combine with orange daylilies and lysimachia to give hotter effects. Finding the right place for some hostas is complicated by the fact that they change colour as the season progresses. *H. fortunei* var. *aureomarginata* begins spectacularly in spring with bright leaves edged with gold, but by mid-season it is decidedly less painted. The middle fades and the edge darkens until the leaf is two-tone green, pleasant but a good deal less striking than it was at its jazzy debut. A large-leaved hosta used in the foreground of a planting scheme with something feathery behind – an astilbe, perhaps, or a fern – creates a useful optical effect, changing one's perception and altering the perspective so the border seems deeper than it really is. Brightly coloured foliage in the foreground, with dimmer, shadowy, greyer ones behind, will have the same effect.

Variegated shrubs need even more careful placing than herbaceous plants, but a dogwood such as *Cornus controversa* 'Variegata' has the potential to be the most beautiful thing in your garden when it begins to leaf up in spring; the foliage is pale and fluttery, each light green leaf with an irregular creamy edge. It is built like a wedding cake, with flat tiers of finely twigged branches reaching out from the central trunk. The whole thing is so light, airy and beautifully constructed that anything too bossy will distract from its elegance, but there will be room for a quiet underplanting of mossy green woodruff (*Galium odoratum*; see p.72), snowdrops or Christmas roses (*Helleborus niger*). The dogwoods are gentle with their variegated effects. *Cornus alba* 'Elegantissima' is less elegant in overall form, but the foliage – pale grey-green, broadly edged with white – is better for picking. It is an undemanding shrub that, if allowed, will spread to make a thicket of stems. In winter light, the bark stands out, smooth, dark red. This dogwood grows without complaint on a wide variety of soils, acid or alkaline, waterlogged or dry. Cut some of the stems hard back in early spring to encourage new growth, which will have larger leaves and brighter bark than that on the older growths.

Cotoneaster atropurpureus 'Variegatus' has a completely different habit: ground-hugging, two-dimensional, a variegated version of the well-known herringbone cotoneaster (*C. horizontalis*). It does not flower or fruit as freely as its cousin, nor is it as vigorous, but it is much more stylish in leaf. These are light grey-green with cream margins, outlined in deep pink. It looks lovely with scillas poking through its flat branches in spring, and it provides a leavening foreground to a rather plain-leaved shrub such as *Rhododendron luteum* (see p.86). Use it at the front of a shrub border where it can stretch out (slowly) over a path and where you can admire its quiet, self-sufficient symmetry.

The lax arching stems of *Fuchsia magellanica* var. *gracilis* 'Versicolor' grow up to about 1.2 m (4 ft) tall and come into leaf quite late, but they will continue to produce both flowers and foliage until cut down by frost. The leaves are a soft, restful, greyish-green, irregularly edged with cream; early in the season they are sometimes flushed over with pale pink. The foliage is a superb foil for the slender scarlet and purple flowers dangling from the stems. Occasionally shoots revert to a plain deep green, and you must cut these out as soon as you see them. They have more vigour than the variegated ones and, left untouched, will take over. These fuchsias prefer full sun but will give a decent performance in light shade. Tall white spires of late summer-flowering galtonias will happily push through the lax growth of the fuchsia, and the two make an elegant pairing.

Throw Away the Rule Book

New gardeners desperately want rules to help them make sense of what they need to do in the garden. But the wonderful thing about gardening is that each year, plants behave differently, as they respond to the conditions around them. One summer they might have to cope with a drought. Sometimes they will be tripped up by a particularly prolonged bout of freezing weather. Rules are not as important as principles. If you understand the principle of why, for instance, you should not set out tender exotics or bedding plants too early in the year, then you know when you can bend the general rules.

You need to understand the growth patterns of particular plants too, in order to get the best out of them. Take the dark-leaved cow parsley (*Anthriscus sylvestris* 'Ravenswing'), a lovely plant if you see it early in the growing season, when its foliage, dark and sumptuous, is at its best. But then it collapses, like its wild relative, so it is no use expecting it to perform with plants that peak in high summer. It is a creature of late spring and early summer only, marvellous in a wild-inspired scheme with another cow parsleyish plant (actually a type of chervil), *Chaerophyllum hirsutum* 'Roseum', with lilac-mauve flowers. You will get the same relaxed effect if you use the anthriscus with a fancy form of Jacob's ladder, such as *Polemonium* 'Sonia's Bluebell', which has paler blue flowers and darker, more bronzed foliage than the species. Another good companion is sisyrinchium, which gives upright sword-shaped, iris-like leaves in places where irises would not be happy. The prettiest of the tribe is a small, cream-striped sisyrinchium called *S. striatum* 'Aunt May'. It bears pale creamy flowers on top of stiff, fan-like foliage, no more than 30 cm (12 in) high.

Gradually, you begin to learn about connecting various events in a bed or a border, joining up separate incidents and groups to make a single flowing tapestry of plants. In this enterprise, you need to learn who your best friends are. They will be big, soft billowing plants like catmint, good enough to be stars themselves but also capable of reaching out and joining hands with other plants around, plants that were not part of the original group you had set the catmint with. Catmint is an excellent buffer plant, because it makes soft mounds of growth, and its texture is matt and gentle. The foliage is good from spring, when it first appears, right up to autumn, when it begins to look tired and worn, as well it might after six months on show. *Nepeta racemosa* 'Walker's Low' (see p.152) is a richly generous catmint that will grow 60 cm (24 in) up as well as out.

Perhaps when you first put in that catmint, you were still in a swoony state about the white garden at Sissinghurst, Kent (though you will grow out of that, sooner or later; sooner is better). You bought a handsome white phlox, carefully choosing one of the *Phlox maculata* types rather than the more common *Phlox paniculata*, because the former is not so prone to attack by eelworm. The phlox does all that you had hoped, flowering in luxuriant columns rather than terminal pyramids, but you begin to wonder whether the colour scheme – tasteful pale greyish-blue and ultra-tasteful white – isn't, well, a bit limiting. You have been reading a book about foliage in the garden, and you have been told you need some important leaves somewhere in what you are now thinking of as your composition. For leaves, read hostas. You decide to be daring and warm the scheme up a bit and choose a goldish sort of hosta rather than a white variegated one. Because you are feeling impatient, you splash out on three hostas, perhaps 'Fragrant Gold' or 'Lemon Lime' (see p.122), and plant them by the phlox. The whole group swings instantly into a different mode. The warming happens. The balance shifts.

Then, having enjoyed these plants all the way from late spring to autumn, you begin to worry about the yawning gap that is going to stretch from autumn round to the following late spring. The three plants you have so far brought together will take you through a long season, passing the baton from one to the other as the months move on, but they still leave you with nothing for early spring. Anemones are the answer: the fat-stemmed, chubby De Caen Group ones. Planted in autumn, these will give you three months of spring flowers in white, pale blue, purple, pink and magenta, along with bright green, ferny foliage. Exuberance is what you need in spring, and anemones have that in abundance. They are so free-flowering that you can pick a fresh potful every week and still not see gaps in the display. Now you are beginning to weave the blanket that will eventually stretch to cover all your garden with a shifting pattern of flowers and leaves. The catmint and the phlox, the hostas and the anemones make a web, which will reach out to touch other webs that you will be creating in neighbouring patches of ground. Before you know it, you will have a joined-up garden. No gardener ever wants the months of late spring and early summer, with their erupting affirmations of life, ever to finish. Making sure there is more still to come softens the blow.

The shuttlecock fern (*Matteuccia struthiopteris*) erupts with magnificent drama in Rosemary's Wood at Bressingham Gardens, Diss, Norfolk, UK. Spread below is a pale carpet of *Scilla bithynica*.

Here is an outrageously wonderful allium, flowering in June but hanging on to its huge spherical seed head well into winter. Silvered, these make dramatic Christmas baubles. Half of the pinkish-mauve flowers are clasped quite close to the centre of the orb, while the other half zoom out on long, pinkish-green stalks like a firework exploding. At maturity, the heads make a complete globe and can measure 40 cm (16 in) across. Half the height of this allium is in the stem, half in the head itself, so it is slightly top-heavy and may need some discreet support.

To be seen at its best, the umbels need air about them. Use the feather reed grass (*Calamagrostis)* as a backdrop, not too close, and interplant the clumps with sturdy blue camassias. This grass is earlier into flower than many and depending on the season, may overlap with the allium. Although the camassias will disappear, both the grass and the sculptural seed heads of the allium will remain through autumn into winter, providing a splendid contrast with each other. The allium is not reliably perennial, but that is not a good enough reason to do without it.

Allium schubertii + *Camassia leichtlinii* subsp. *suksdorfii* Caerulea Group / *Calamagrostis* × *acutiflora* 'Karl Foerster'

(1) *Allium schubertii*

HEIGHT: 45–60 cm (18–24 in)

SPREAD: 20 cm (8 in)

FLOWERING TIME: Early summer

STAR QUALITIES: The most dramatic of all alliums, both in the size of its flower and its structure. Handsome, long-lasting seed heads.

ALTERNATIVES: *A. cristophii* is built in a similar way, but the flower head is smaller and more compact. They are different from the majority of alliums, which mostly have tall, uncluttered stems with a purple blob on top. Favourites among this tribe include *A.* 'Ambassador', 'Purple Sensation' and 'Globemaster', which has extra-large heads.

(2) *Camassia leichtlinii* subsp. *suksdorfii* Caerulea Group

With careful planting, you should be able to place the camassias so their foliage to some extent disguises that of the alliums, which so often is at its worst when the flower is at its best. Camassias of the Caerulea Group build up into magnificent clumps about 80 cm (32 in) tall, with long-lasting lavender-blue flowers. They do not set seed but depend entirely on the bulbs underground splitting and increasing.

(3) *Calamagrostis* × *acutiflora* 'Karl Foerster' (Feather reed grass)

By early summer, this stiffly upright grass is already sending up flowering stems of pinkish-bronze that gradually fade to buff. With the onset of winter, the arching foliage dies away, but the strong seed stems remain standing. Leave them until early spring before cutting them down to the ground. The group can be extended by adding later-flowering herbaceous perennials such as veronicastrum and thalictrum to partner the grass.

1

2

3

This is a group in the modern style: not exactly minimal, but cool and restrained. The invaluable geranium 'Bill Wallis' provides intermittent splashes of glowing purple between the muted tones of the other two plants. The star attraction is the *Allium siculum* (formerly *Nectaroscordum siculum*) – an angular, strange piece of sculpture, whether in flower or in seed. Each stem grows to about 75 cm (30 in) tall, topped by a tall, pointed bud wrapped in a papery sheath. This breaks open into a drooping head of up to thirty flowers, striped in cream and maroon. Individually they are small, but because they open in succession, each head lasts a long time. Bumblebees adore them, and these strange beauties provide plenty of opportunity for them to forage. The seed pods are a great feature, because they turn upwards as they dry, and the rigid stems rise like minimalist candelabra from the leafy underpinning of grass and geranium. Once, the nectaroscordum was in a family of its own, containing only itself. Now it has been shifted into the big family of alliums. This trio also features a particularly elegant grass. Designers love grasses for their architectural form and their seed heads, which persist long into winter. The tufted hair grass (*Deschampsia*), like all grasses, has a long season of interest, and its spikes of flower will provide a fine contrast with the nectaroscordum's seed heads. The most daring gasp of colour will come from the geranium, which will continue to produce a succession of flowers, small but richly coloured, from late spring all the way to early autumn.

Allium siculum + *Deschampsia cespitosa* 'Goldtau' / *Geranium pyrenaicum* 'Bill Wallis'

(1) *Allium siculum*

HEIGHT: 1.2 m (4 ft)

SPREAD: 10 cm (4 in)

FLOWERING TIME: Early to mid-summer

STAR QUALITIES: Tall, stiff stems bear heads of bell-shaped flowers, hanging bashfully downwards. They are a strange colour – not quite pink, not quite green or grey.

ALTERNATIVES: The subspecies *dioscoridis* is very similar, but there is more purple than pink in the flower heads; a tall allium such as *A.* 'Ambassador' or *A. giganteum* could be used instead.

(2) *Deschampsia cespitosa* 'Goldtau' (Tufted hair grass)

The species is one of the biggest and most beautiful of the grasses, native to Britain and much of the rest of Europe. In the wild, it favours damp, acid soil, producing dense tussocks of narrow, dark leaves and tall, strong flowering stems up to 1.2 m (4 ft). 'Goldtau' makes elegant plumes of tiny purplish-green flowers; by autumn, the spikes fade to pale creamy yellow.

(3) *Geranium pyrenaicum* 'Bill Wallis'

The wild species is widespread in western Europe, with flowers of a deep mauve-pink. 'Bill Wallis', named after the Cambridgeshire nurseryman who selected it, has much more telling flowers of a rich, saturated purple. The habit of this geranium is to sprawl comfortably between its companions, where it will produce a long succession of its small, veined flowers.

3

2

Aquilegias are such shameless cross-breeders, it is difficult to keep named varieties such as 'Blue Barlow' true to type. Self-seeding is to be encouraged, though, as new beauties crop up each season. The Barlow series of double aquilegias started with promiscuous, pink 'Nora Barlow', which produced a huge family of granny's bonnets, all in different colours. These types are much easier to keep in cultivation than the long-spurred types, but you need both. 'Yellow Queen', selected from the North American native, *Aquilegia chrysantha*, has exceptionally long, elegant spurs and would look equally lovely with the dianthus. All aquilegias like heavy soil, are happy in sun or shade and have deeply cut greyish foliage, which is an asset even when the plant is not flowering. The plants can be tidied up in late summer, when they will produce fresh mounds of foliage, of the same greyish hue as the pinks. The crocus will take care of early spring, and the pinks, the modern kinds at least, will go on flowering sporadically until early autumn.

Aquilegia vulgaris var. *stellata* 'Blue Barlow' + *Crocus sublimis* 'Tricolor' / *Dianthus* 'Musgrave's Pink'

---

1. *Aquilegia vulgaris* var. *stellata* 'Blue Barlow' (Columbine, Granny's bonnet)

HEIGHT: 90 cm (36 in)

SPREAD: 45 cm (18 in)

FLOWERING TIME: Late spring to early summer

STAR QUALITIES: Mounds of elegant, greyish foliage, a good foil for early bulbs. Double pompon flowers with narrow petals of a clear, bright blue.

ALTERNATIVES: 'Nora Barlow' is a double with rich pink flowers tipped with green and cream; 'Nivea' has pure white flowers; the McKana Group produces long-spurred flowers, beautiful but more difficult to keep than *A. vulgaris* types.

2. *Crocus sublimis* 'Tricolor'

An early (February–March), sturdily upright crocus with an outstanding flower. It is deep purple, with a white band separating it from the yellow at the base of the bloom. Dark bronze runs down the throat into the sheath. This is a neat, compact crocus, slightly reluctant to open wide, but remarkable for the intensity of its colour.

3. *Dianthus* 'Musgrave's Pink'

This pink is sometimes called 'Green Eyes' because of its neat, acid-green centre. It is an elegant pink, though not as long in its flowering as other more modern varieties. Clove-scented *D.* 'Alice' is equally good, as is the old-fashioned 'Dad's Favourite'.

2

3

Here is a relaxed planting to bring the hot hillsides of the western Mediterranean to mind, the shrubby cistus surrounded by self-seeding annuals that will also be happy on a gravelly, sun-struck slope in the garden. The cistus is evergreen, with dark, leathery, pointed leaves mounding slowly up on a bush about 1.5 m (5 ft) high. In early summer, this sombre creation lights up with large, white, papery flowers, at least 7 cm (3 in) across. Each of the petals has a distinctive dark maroon blotch at the centre, arranged around a boss of bright stamens.

In this grouping, the cistus is joined by opium poppies and the superb annual umbellifer *Orlaya grandiflora*. Both will self-seed, but if they gradually die out, take the opportunity to try a new combination: a sea of bright nasturtiums, perhaps, or a waving field of pale blue love-in-a-mist. For early spring, you could add crocus or early-flowering, low-growing species tulips. The effect should be of plants that have brought themselves to this happy spot naturally.

Cistus × *cyprius* + *Orlaya grandiflora* / *Papaver somniferum*

(1) *Cistus* × *cyprius* (Sun rose)

HEIGHT: 1.5 m (5 ft)

SPREAD: 1.5 m (5 ft)

FLOWERING TIME: Early summer

STAR QUALITIES: Masses of eye-catching, papery white flowers with a dark maroon blotch at the base of each petal. Neat, dark green leaves.

ALTERNATIVES: *C.* × *hybridus* is shorter and has pure white flowers without the dark blotch; *C.* × *purpureus* has crinkled flowers of dark pink.

(2) *Orlaya grandiflora*

An enchanting annual with big flat heads of lopsided white flowers, two longish petals hanging down from a bunch of short ones. It is, in many ways, easier to use than its umbellifer cousin, ammi, because it is shorter, and the bright green filigree foliage is prettier. The best results come from seed sown direct in autumn, which will provide an early show. If you sow more seed in spring, the display will continue until late summer.

(3) *Papaver somniferum* (Opium poppy)

This is one of the most generous of annual flowers, with splendid glaucous foliage, beautiful flowers, either double or single, and dramatic pepperpot seed heads. Colours range over the pink and purple spectrum: *P.* 'Black Beauty' is a deep maroon double, packed to bursting with petals, and 'Lilac Pompon' is a pale pink flower, shaggier than a poodle's topknot. If your aim is to produce a more natural look, go for the single 'Dark Plum', its clear plum-purple petals with dark blotches at their base echoing those of the cistus.

2

3

Pinks and greys ebb and flow through this group of plants, centred on the fine dicentra 'Stuart Boothman'. If you want to make the whole group larger, use one of the bigger dicentra lookalikes, such as *Lamprocapnos spectabilis*, though you will lose the advantage of the grey foliage, which is perhaps the most attractive element of the whole group. In terms of flowers, the performance will start with the wood anemones, which have the fragile, consumptive air of flowers that are not long for this world. In the hurly-burly of summer, they would not be strong enough to hold their ground, but in spring, there is space for them to languish elegantly. The rhizomes look unpromising – shapeless pieces of fossilized Plasticine – but the transformation from toad to prince is astounding. The dicentra will start as the anemones finish. Though its main season is late spring, it will flower intermittently through the summer too. By that stage, it will have been joined by the beautiful glossy leaves of *Hosta* 'Devon Green'. Like the dicentra, this is a plant whose foliage is just as welcome as its flowers.

Dicentra 'Stuart Boothman' + *Hosta* 'Devon Green' / *Anemone nemorosa* 'Robinsoniana'

(1) *Dicentra* 'Stuart Boothman' (Bleeding heart)

HEIGHT: 30 cm (12 in)

SPREAD: 40 cm (16 in)

FLOWERING TIME: Mid-spring to early summer

STAR QUALITIES: Beautiful, finely cut, grey foliage; pink flowers that hang like little lockets along the stems.

ALTERNATIVES: *D.* 'Langtrees' has grey foliage with white flowers; 'Bacchanal' has dark crimson flowers, the darkest of this tribe, but the foliage is less striking; *Lamprocapnos spectabilis* (formerly *Dicentra spectabilis)* has far showier flowering stems, but the foliage is green; *L. spectabilis* 'Alba' makes a big plant, up to 1.2 m (4 ft) high, with showy white flowers dangling from the stems.

(2) *Hosta* 'Devon Green'

A sport of 'Halcyon', found by Roger and Ann Bowden at their hosta nursery in Devon, in the southwest of England, 'Devon Green' develops into a dense mound of dark green leaves, wonderfully rich and glossy. It grows to about 50 cm (20 in) high and produces its pale lavender flowers towards the end of summer. Blue-leaved 'Halcyon' (see p.128) is an alternative, echoing the cool, metallic tone of the dicentra. It is taller than 'Devon Green', but its spikes of flower are of a similar colour.

(3) *Anemone nemorosa* 'Robinsoniana' (Wood anemone, Windflower)

From this anemone come delicate, very pale blue-mauve windflowers, 13 cm (5 in) high, with darkish green, finely cut foliage. 'Virescens' is a bizarrely intriguing form in which all the petals have turned themselves into tiny, divided green leaves to make a rather appealing mossy mop. Wood anemones should not be planted too deep: 3 cm (1 in) of earth on top of the rhizomes is plenty. Moist, cool, shady, humus-rich soil is what they like best.

3

1

2

Ferns, like spurges, are reliable bankers, provided you can give them the cool conditions they like, and they make superb long-term companions for more ephemeral plants. For looks, you cannot do better than *Dryopteris wallichiana* – tall, elegant, formally and soberly suited but without a hint of stuffiness. The fronds, uncurling in late spring, arrange themselves with the easy poise that comes of 400 million years of breeding. 'No flowers? No fruit? No smell?' you may ask. No, none of those. This is the horticultural equivalent of the plain, very expensive little black dress. *D. filix-mas* is a common fern in the temperate zones of the northern hemisphere, but *D. wallichiana* comes from Central Asia and has a faintly dangerous air about it, unusual in ferns, intensified by the dark, thick fur that clothes the back of the stems. Fill the ground around the fern with masses of aconites (*Eranthis*) to provide delight in early spring. The stems of Solomon's seal (*Polygonatum*) will rear up elegantly between the clumps of fern (until they are chewed to bits by voracious sawfly). This relaxed group, wild at heart, is best suited to the kind of shade cast by a deciduous tree, which will allow early spring sun to reach the aconites and tickle open their bright flowers.

Dryopteris wallichiana + *Eranthis hyemalis* / *Polygonatum × hybridum*

(1) *Dryopteris wallichiana* (Wallich's wood fern)

HEIGHT: 90 cm (36 in)

SPREAD: 75 cm (30 in)

FLOWERING TIME: Deciduous fern

STAR QUALITIES: Elegant shuttlecock shape; midribs thickly covered with dark brown scales that look like fur. The fronds, when they first emerge in spring, are brilliant yellowish-green.

ALTERNATIVES: *D. filix-mas*, the common male fern, is a tougher member of the family but does not have the wonderful hairy midribs of *D. wallichiana*.

(2) *Eranthis hyemalis* (Winter aconite)

Aconites are one of the earliest bulbs to flower, racing neck-and-neck with snowdrops to appear in late winter. Fat juicy stems, 5–10 cm (2–4 in) long, end in ruffs of bright green leaves that surround the bright yellow, globe-shaped flowers. The tubers hate to be dried out. Try to get hold of plants 'in the green', just after they have finished flowering. Planted like this, they will establish much more reliably than from dry tubers.

(3) *Polygonatum × hybridum* (Solomon's seal)

An easy-going woodland plant which will do without sun if necessary. It has an elegant habit of growth, the stems thrusting through the ground in mid-spring and then bending gently over, bearing, by late spring, narrow, creamy white flowers that hang all along the stems. In cool, humus-rich soil, Solomon's seal spreads quickly by underground rhizomes.

2

1

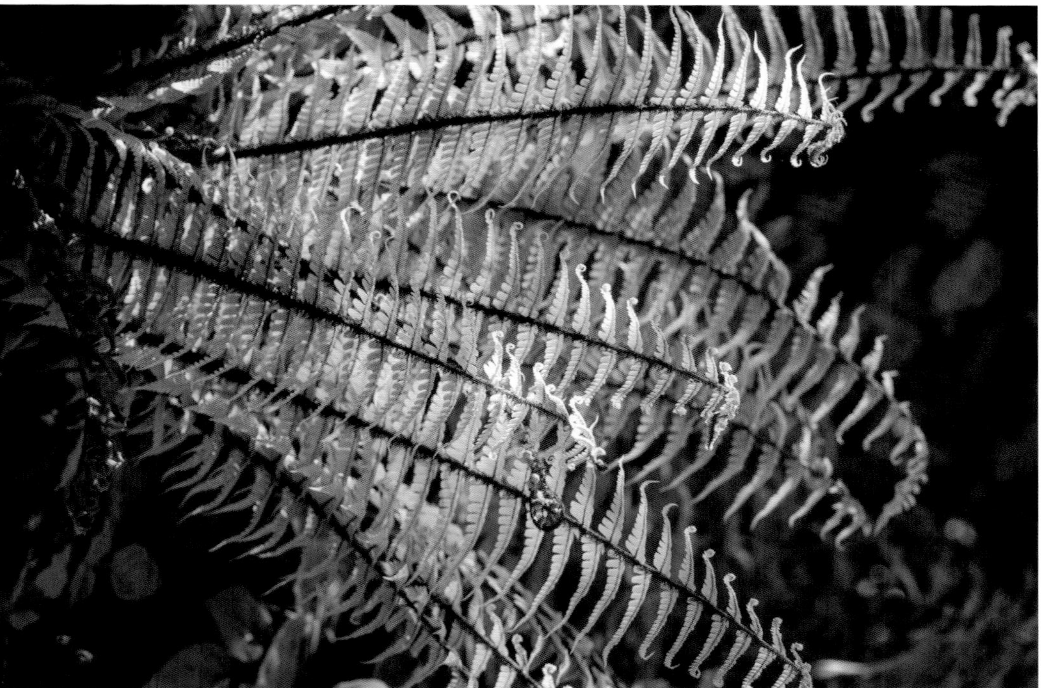

3

The star here is a splendid foliage plant, a solid clump with many stems springing from the base. The stems have a biennial habit, making leaves in their first year; then, in the spring of their second year, most produce great domes of sulphurous yellow-green flowers. Meanwhile, new shoots are being produced from the base, so there is an ever-rolling supply of new growth and no off-season gap. This spurge comes from rocky places in the Mediterranean, so will appreciate a sunny spot in the garden. In high summer, the sound of the seeds exploding will make you think you are on a Greek hillside. Because it self-seeds so freely, the species is very variable. Some, such as *Euphorbia* 'John Tomlinson', have noticeably fine heads of flower, while others, such as 'Portuguese Velvet', are usefully compact. Each season, cut out the stems that have flowered. In choosing agapanthus, you need to think about hardiness, height, generosity and time of flowering as well as colour, which can be anything from deep blue to ice white. *Agapanthus* 'Isis' flowers mid-season with deep blue blooms and is not too tall (65 cm/26 in). The lavender blue, double-flowered cranesbill will be at its peak between the last gasps of the spurge flowers and the beginning of the agapanthus. Cut back the clump to encourage a late season, more sporadic flowering.

Euphorbia characias subsp. *wulfenii* + *Agapanthus* 'Isis' / *Geranium pratense* 'Plenum Violaceum'

(1) *Euphorbia characias* subsp. *wulfenii*

HEIGHT: 1.2 m (4 ft)

SPREAD: 1.2 m (4 ft)

FLOWERING TIME: Early spring to early summer

STAR QUALITIES: Landmark evergreen plant with superb, glaucous foliage held in whorls round the stem. Big flower heads of intense greenish-yellow.

ALTERNATIVES: Foliage in some types is bluer than others, and some varieties have particularly showy flowers; *E.* 'John Tomlinson' has big, almost spherical flower heads, nearly 40 cm (16 in) long; 'Tasmanian Tiger' is dramatically variegated.

(2) *Agapanthus* 'Isis'

A rough rule of thumb in choosing agapanthus is that the broader the leaf, the more tender the variety. 'Isis' is hardy. Species have been intricately interbred to produce more than 500 varieties. Most make a rounded head of trumpet flowers, but *A. inapertus* has long-tubed flowers that hang down from the top of the stem. Provenance is important: check that the plant you buy has come from division, not from seed, which will not necessarily produce a plant like its parent. The straplike leaves of the agapanthus will provide a fine contrast with the foliage of the spurge.

(3) *Geranium pratense* 'Plenum Violaceum' (Cranesbill)

Deeply divided leaves make a clump up to 60 cm (24 in) high and wide. In the right conditions, the foliage colours well in autumn. 'Plenum Violaceum' has double flowers of a wonderful deep violet-blue, which come out in high summer and last for several weeks, longer than the single-flowered types. Arrange some twiggy sticks for the lax stems to scramble through.

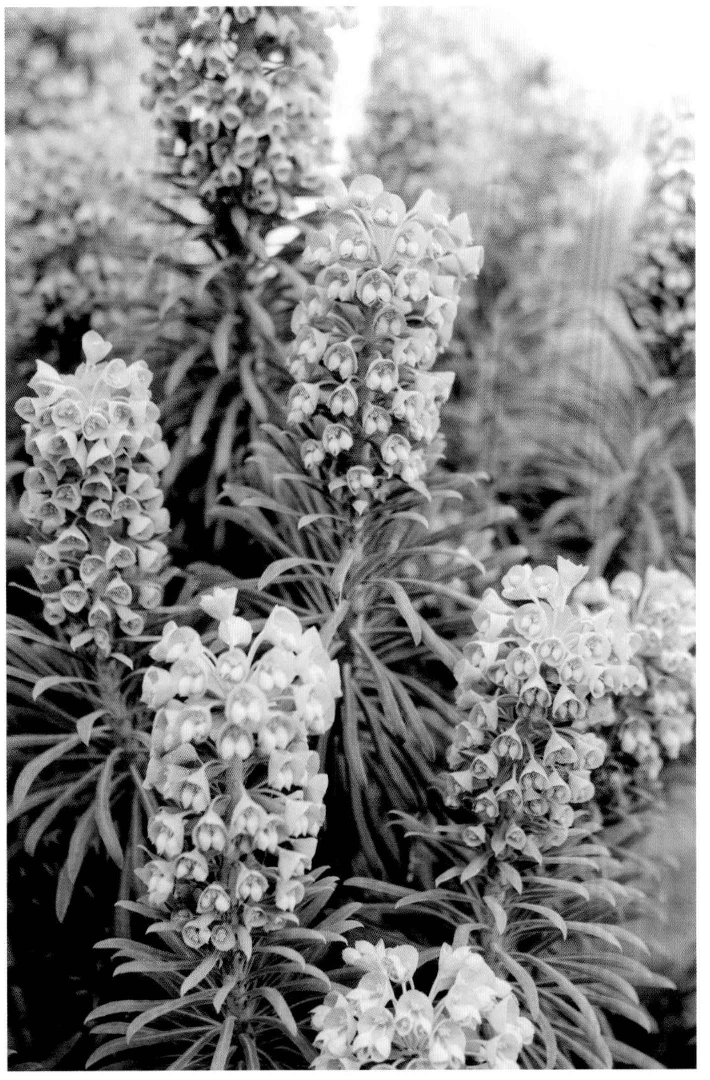

Exochorda × macrantha 'The Bride' is one of the most generous of flowering shrubs, with lax branches almost weighed down with scented white blossom. It flowers on growth made the previous season, and it seems that every bud on every twig is intent on producing its own show-stopping extravaganza. This hybrid generally grows as wide as it is high, and any necessary pruning needs to be done as soon as the shrub has finished flowering. This will leave it as much time as possible to make the new growth on which the following year's display will depend. Remaining leaves may develop yellow and orange tints as autumn arrives. Underneath, you can spread low groundcover plants such as woodruff and saxifrage. After its spring flowering, the foliage of woodruff (*Galium odoratum*) remains fresh and green throughout summer and autumn. To extend the flowering season, use a saxifrage such as *Saxifraga fortunei* 'Silver Velvet', which does not produce its white flowers until late summer. In form, the two plants make a strongly contrasting pair, the one with small, fine leaves arranged in starlike whorls, the other with big, rounded, fleshy leaves, flushed reddish-purple on the underside.

Exochorda × macrantha 'The Bride'	+	*Saxifraga fortunei* 'Silver Velvet'
		Galium odoratum

(1) *Exochorda × macrantha* 'The Bride'

HEIGHT: 1.5–2.5 m (5–8 ft)

SPREAD: 1.5–2.5 m (5–8 ft)

FLOWERING TIME: Late spring to early summer

STAR QUALITIES: A compact, but wonderfully generous shrub, its arching branches weighed down with scented white flowers.

ALTERNATIVES: 'Niagara' is a cross between 'The Bride' and another species, *E. racemosa*. It is more compact than 'The Bride' but not as elegant.

(2) *Saxifraga fortunei* 'Silver Velvet'

This saxifrage is unusual in that it produces its white flowers in late summer rather than spring. They are charmingly lopsided, with three short petals and two long ones hanging down below. The foliage is handsome, with dark burgundy, fleshy leaves, glossy, rounded and lobed, sometimes usefully evergreen but only in mild winters. Flowering stems reach to about 30 cm (12 in). There are several named varieties – some, like *S.* 'Cherry Pie', with bright pink flowers, some, such as 'Black Ruby', with glossy, exceedingly dark foliage.

(3) *Galium odoratum* (Woodruff)

Mats of bright whorled leaves give the effect of sprightly moss topped with tiny, scented white flowers, the four petals arranged in the shape of a cross. Though it gallops about enthusiastically, woodruff is not a bully and can easily be plucked out where it is not wanted. It will spread into a clump about 30 cm (12 in) across, but even at flowering time, it is no more than 15 cm (6 in) high.

3

This trio has little but flower power to offer the gardener – but what flowers! From time to time it is good for the soul to abandon precepts about foliage and texture and form and succumb to pure hedonism. Irises are made for hedonists. The name comes from the Greek goddess of the rainbow, and the flowers make a reasonable job of covering the spectrum. Only a true red is missing, and the family is strongest on the blue, indigo, violet end of the scale. The kind of place bearded irises grow best is a narrow border, such as might run alongside a pergola or a path, where they can be in full sun but not have to share their space with too many other plants. Big bearded irises, such as 'Jane Phillips', are not generally good mixers, as they need the sun on their rhizomes to bake them. A sprinkling of some light-limbed annual, such as love-in-a-mist (*Nigella*) would work, but the ideal companions are bulbs, which, performing at different seasons to the iris, then put themselves neatly away until they are next wanted. Bearded irises's own flowering season is early summer, so to spread the flowering time, use autum-flowering bulbs as well as spring-flowering ones.

Iris 'Jane Phillips' + *Crocus speciosus* / *Tulipa orphanidea* Whittallii Group

---

(1) *Iris* 'Jane Phillips'

HEIGHT: 1 m (3 ft)

SPREAD: 60 cm (24 in)

FLOWERING TIME: Late spring to early summer

STAR QUALITIES: Gorgeous sky-blue flowers on long, strong stems. Sword foliage gives interest before the flowers appear.

ALTERNATIVES: Tall bearded irises are the most stately, but there are medium and short hybrids available too. *I.* 'Raspberry Blush' (intermediate) has flowers of a dusky pale pink; 'Hocus Pocus' (dwarf) has lilac-blue uprights with coppery falls.

(2) *Crocus speciosus*

We think of crocus as predominantly spring-flowering bulbs, but this is one of a wonderful group of species that appear in autumn. The solitary flowers, up to 5 cm (2 in) long, appear before the leaves. The species is a gorgeous, rich, violet-blue, but there is a form, 'Albus', that is pure white. 'Conqueror' has deep blue flowers. In the right conditions – well-drained ground in sun or light shade – these crocuses will spread rapidly by seed and offsets.

(3) *Tulipa orphanidea* Whittallii Group

Here you have an outstanding tulip, no more than 30 cm (12 in) high, with neat, pointed petals. The colour is a burnt orange caramel, very distinct and unusual. The outer petals are smaller than the inner ones and are flushed with a pale creamy buff on the reverse. The flower makes a perfect rounded bud, with all the petals meeting at a sharp point in the middle. There is a smoky, indeterminate basal blotch, greenish-black with a yellow halo, the dark colour drifting slightly up the veins of the petals, like watercolours on wet paper.

2

3

The Siberian irises form thick, herbaceous clumps in the garden, producing their early-summer flowers in a wide range of blues, mauves, whites and yellows. *Iris sibirica* 'Flight of Butterflies' has smaller blooms than many of its cousins, but they are freely produced and most exquisitely marked. The overall colour is a clear, bright blue, but the falls are white, edged and delicately veined in the same blue. The selinum provides a lacy contrast, the foliage emerging in spring as intricately divided as a fern's. When fully grown, the stems will reach 1.5 m (5 ft) and in some forms are stained a deep reddish-purple. In high summer they are joined by flat white umbels of flowers, like a very high-class cow parsley. These flower heads can be as much as 20 cm (8 in) across, airy and graceful. The foliage of the iris and the selinum will act as a buffer and support for the lilies, which can soar up between them. White *Lilium* 'Casa Blanca' is heavily scented, a bonus you should not ignore.

Iris sibirica 'Flight of Butterflies' + *Lilium* 'Casa Blanca' / *Selinum wallichianum*

① *Iris sibirica* 'Flight of Butterflies'

HEIGHT: 90 cm (36 in)

SPREAD: 60 cm (24 in)

FLOWERING TIME: Early summer

STAR QUALITIES: Tough, hardy, easy to grow. Elegant, intricately veined flowers, like heraldic fleur-de-lys.

ALTERNATIVES: There are masses of different varieties of *I. sibirica*. 'Berlin Ruffles' has deep blue flowers with silver-edged falls; 'Dreaming Yellow' has white standards and slightly ruffled, creamy yellow falls; 'Harpswell Happiness' has broad-petalled flowers of pure white.

② *Lilium* 'Casa Blanca' (Lily)

A trumpet-shaped lily, up to 1 m (3 ft) tall, with big white flowers, washed over on the backs of the petals with the palest of pinks. The flowers face boldly outwards, all the better for sniffing, for this is a richly scented lily, especially at night. The petals are broad and slightly reflexed, making a wide-faced flower with the stamens looping out in a dramatic way. The inner surface of each petal is slightly puckered, standing up in a series of small points.

③ *Selinum wallichianum*

A magnificent plant of the cow parsley family, called umbellifers because they have big, flattish heads of flowers like umbrellas. Some, like those of the annual umbellifer *Visnaga daucoides* (formerly, *Ammi visnaga*, see p.144), are dense and tight. Selinum's flower heads are lacy and spacey, held airily above the bright green foliage. This is a beautiful plant, generously lending its considerable attributes to enhance whatever other plant you choose to grow with it.

3

2

1

You can use the royal fern, *Osmunda regalis*, to great effect in a garden, provided the soil is damp. It does not mind sun as long as its roots are moist and cool, but remember that it takes a little while to build up to its mature regal stature of 2 m (6 ft). The standard royal fern is grandly leafy, the green fronds turning clear butter-yellow in autumn before they die down. In the wild, these are plants of the water margin – ditches in western Ireland are full of them – and they will not thrive without this gentle dampness around them at all times. They prefer acid soils to alkaline ones, but that is not as important a requirement as wetness. Use royal ferns with plants that like the same conditions; they are natural companions for rodgersias of all kinds, and they also look splendid pierced by the tall sword foliage of yellow-flowered flag iris.

Osmunda regalis + *Iris pseudacorus* 'Variegata' / *Rodgersia pinnata* 'Superba'

① *Osmunda regalis* (Royal fern)

HEIGHT: 2 m (6 ft)

SPREAD: 2 m (6 ft)

FLOWERING TIME: Deciduous fern

STAR QUALITIES: Bright green fronds uncurl in late spring to produce clumps of foliage at least 1 m (3 ft) high. In summer, tall stems bearing clusters of rusty brown spores appear between the leaves.

ALTERNATIVES: 'Cristata' has leaves with crested tips; 'Purpurascens' has foliage flushed in its early stage with bronze-purple.

② *Iris pseudacorus* 'Variegata'

This is the handsome variegated form of the native flag iris, which in the wild, like the royal fern, is most often found in damp ditches or at the margins of ponds and streams. The markedly upright, sword leaves provide a splendid contrast with the fern's fronds, and in summer there is the added bonus of bright yellow flowers, which come out in succession up the stems.

③ *Rodgersia pinnata* 'Superba'

A splendid foliage plant with leaves like great hands, at least 30 cm (12 in) across, borne on strong stems. The flowers come late in the season and are carried well above the foliage in fluffy spikes of brilliant pink, rather like an astilbe's. 'Superba' gets its name because the leaves are particularly well-burnished, like old leather.

1

2

3

Some plants are gaunt in a good way. This shrubby peony is upright and sparsely branched and certainly has an element of gauntness – but only in winter, after its leaves have dropped, and then you might equally well describe it as splendidly sculptural. The leaves are superb, deeply dissected and darkly shining. From late spring to early summer, they are joined by gently drooping flowers, 5–6 cm (2 in) across. In the best form these are a dark maroon-red, each with a central boss of golden stamens. This peony is a glorious creature, happy in partial shade and spacy enough in its structure to allow tall stems of *Gladiolus murielae* to find their way through to flower in late summer. Where it is comfortable, the peony may well sucker, which is, in this case, to be encouraged. The more you have of the beautiful foliage, the better. Introduce a few clumps of *Agastache* 'Blackadder' on the sunny perimeter of the peony's spread. The blue, fluffy spikes are a great magnet for bees, and their flowering will overlap with that of the gladiolus.

Paeonia delavayi + *Agastache* 'Blackadder' / *Gladiolus murielae*

1 *Paeonia delavayi*

HEIGHT: 2 m (6 ft)

SPREAD: 1.2 m (4 ft)

FLOWERING TIME: Late spring to early summer

STAR QUALITIES: A splendid landmark in a garden, with handsome, long-lasting foliage that provides an excellent backdrop for later flowering companions. The flowers, though relatively small, are delicately presented and, in the deep red form, of a wonderful colour.

ALTERNATIVES: *P. rockii* is perhaps the most lauded of the shrubby tree peonies, with huge, crinkled white blooms blotched in the centre with maroon; *P. ludlowii* has single flowers of a vivid yellow.

2 *Agastache* 'Blackadder' (Giant hyssop)

This is an ornamental version of the medicinal herb, attracting bees, butterflies and masses of hoverflies to its stubby blue flower spikes. Flowering continues all summer, but the plant is only borderline hardy, and a tough winter may prove too much for it. It is worth the gamble, though. The foliage is aromatic and smells faintly of aniseed. Leave the dead stems over winter to provide some protection against frost. If you are not a gambler, use a salvia such as *S. nemorosa* 'Ostfriesland' instead.

3 *Gladiolus murielae*

Foliage and flower stems are roughly the same height (1 m / 3 ft), with the slightly drooping flowers opening in succession up the stem. There may be as many as eight on each one, so flowering lasts a long time. The blooms look nothing like a typical gladiolus: the six petals flare out from a long, narrow tube to make an elegant flower, white blotched with maroon at the centre. Formerly known as *Acidanthera*, they are gorgeously scented, but not reliably hardy. Fortunately, they aren't expensive. Plant more each spring.

2

3

One of the many reasons to choose an Itoh (Intersectional) peony above any of the ordinary herbaceous kinds is that they last longer in flower. They also bear blooms of outrageous size. If you are going to have a peony, you might as well have one that knocks you out with its chutzpah. The name commemorates the Japanese breeder Toichi Itoh, who first crossed herbaceous peonies with shrubby tree peonies to create this magnificent new group, combining the massive, scented flowers and finely cut foliage of tree peonies with the compact habit of a herbaceous peony. The flowers of herbaceous peonies are restricted to various reds, pinks and white, but the Itoh peonies include yellows and apricots too. Mature plants can bear as many as fifty flowers, which come out in succession over at least a month. In autumn the leaves provide a final, defiant display of orange, red and burgundy before they drop cleanly from the plant. The foliage of herbaceous peonies, which just shrivels brownly on the stem, cannot compete. The dark, wild-looking martagon lily overlaps with the peony. The spurge comes later, and later still is the final autumn blaze of the peony foliage.

Paeonia 'Love Affair' + *Euphorbia schillingii* / *Lilium* 'Claude Shride'

① *Paeonia* 'Love Affair'

HEIGHT: 60–90 cm (24–36 in)

SPREAD: 60–90 cm (24–36 in)

FLOWERING TIME: Mid-summer

STAR QUALITIES: 'Love Affair' is pure white, but the Itoh peonies are available in a wide range of colours. The flowers are sterile and last twice as long as those of traditional herbaceous peonies. Foliage colours well in autumn.

ALTERNATIVES: Sherbet-yellow 'Bartzella' was one of the earliest of the Intersectionals to be introduced; 'Cora Louise' is palest pink, with a deep maroon centre.

② *Euphorbia schillingii*

The fine plantsman Tony Schilling, curator of Kew Gardens' outpost Wakehurst Place, in West Sussex, introduced this plant from Nepal, and it quickly rose through the spurge ranks to become one of the five best. It grows up to 1 m (3 ft) tall, making a clump of stems clothed in dark green leaves, each with a pale midrib. In summer these produce typical spurge flower heads of greenish-yellow, which last until mid-autumn. It is deciduous.

③ *Lilium* 'Claude Shride'

'Claude Shride', a hybrid between *L. martagon* and *L. hansonii*, has flowers of deep mahogany-red. It will grow in almost any well-drained soil in full sun or partial shade, with bright green stems up to 1.2m (4 ft) tall and as many as fifty small, nodding Turk's cap flowers hanging from each. They are very small – no more than 4 cm (1 ½ in) across – but the mass makes up for the individual.

3

2

1

Provided its roots stay moist and cool, this beautiful variant of the soft shield fern will grow quite happily in full sun, but it is perhaps seen to best advantage in semi-shade, where it will spread out to make a swirling wheel of foliage, each perfectly constructed green frond supported by a pale brown midrib. Because it is an evergreen, you can set any number of more transitory partners alongside it, each of which it will effortlessly outclass. Flowers may come and go, but ferns such as 'Pulcherriumum Bevis' (discovered by an agricultural labourer named Bevis in a Devon hedge bank) go on for ever. This is a long-lasting group of plants, with both the fern and the spurge providing a twelve-month season of interest. The peak is spring, when first the snowdrop, then the spurge come into flower – but long after they have gone, you will find yourself seeking out the fern.

Polystichum setiferum 'Pulcherrimum Bevis' + *Euphorbia* × *martinii* / *Galanthus* 'Atkinsii'

① *Polystichum setiferum* 'Pulcherrimum Bevis'

HEIGHT: 60–80 cm (24–32 in)

SPREAD: 60–80 cm (24–32 in)

FLOWERING TIME: Evergreen fern

STAR QUALITIES: Beautifully balanced form. Finely divided fronds of exceptional elegance and texture.

ALTERNATIVES: Ferns of the *P. setiferum* Divisilobum Group make more congested clumps, the fronds growing horizontally rather than vertically and often overlapping each other.

② *Euphorbia* × *martinii*

A native of the south of France, this spurge is technically a sub-shrub, rather than a perennial. Its upright stems make clumps of evergreen foliage up to 1 m (3 ft) high, the leaves tinged with a purplish-red. Yellowish-green flowers with bright red centres are borne at the ends of the stems from mid-spring to mid-summer.

③ *Galanthus* 'Atkinsii'

Snowdrop fanciers spend most of late winter and early spring on their knees arguing about the provenance of their pet flowers. The main thing we ordinary mortals notice about 'Atkinsii' is that it is big, growing up to 20 cm (8 in), twice as high as the common snowdrop, *G. nivalis*. There is a heart-shaped green mark at the tip of each inner petal.

2

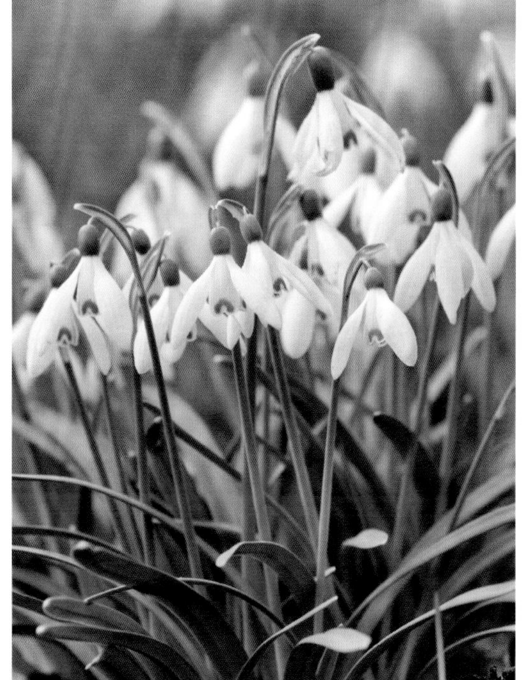

3

The name 'rhododendron' brings to mind a vast shrub with heavy, evergreen leaves and elephantine heads of flower, in terrifying reds or purples. Ditch that image. *R. luteum* is a light-limbed, deciduous shrub that slowly builds into an easy, open beauty. From this framework, in late spring, come glorious trusses of yellow flowers that will scent the entire garden. Moreover, in autumn the whole shrub blazes out in brilliant red, as the foliage shows it can be just as much of an attraction as the flowers. Being a species, this rhododendron has a pleasantly relaxed, wild feeling about it, which you can enhance with companions such as the gorgeous little iris 'Lady Beatrix Stanley', which comes into flower in early spring, before the rhododendron's fat buds have burst. The primula, a species from the Himalayas, is unusual in producing its flowers in late summer, rather than spring.

Rhododendron luteum + *Primula capitata* subsp. *mooreana* / *Iris histrioides* 'Lady Beatrix Stanley'

(1) *Rhododendron luteum*

HEIGHT: 3 m (10 ft)

SPREAD: 3 m (10 ft)

FLOWERING TIME: Late spring to early summer

STAR QUALITIES: Generous in its flowering and prodigious with its scent. Builds into a fine, open structure, with foliage that turns blazing red in autumn.

ALTERNATIVES: *R.* 'Narcissiflorum' is of a similar height and build, with double yellow flowers, almost as well-scented; it too has foliage that colours in autumn.

(2) *Primula capitata* subsp. *mooreana*

A charming, though unfortunately short-lived perennial primula, with foliage that is heavily dusted with a silvery meal. The stems are similarly powdered and bear flattish domes of flower in a rich, deep violet. The colour is all on the outside of the ring, with the centre another floury confection. Be prepared to replace plants every few years, for once you have this appealing primula you will not want to be without it.

(3) *Iris histrioides* 'Lady Beatrix Stanley'

This is one of the most beautiful of all the early-flowering dwarf iris. Overall, the colour is a rich, saturated blue, the throats creamy, with a bright yellow beard running down into the centre of the flower. It flowers only 9 cm (4 in) above the ground and, despite its seeming fragility, is fully hardy. It was introduced into cultivation around 1930 and named after the intimidating editor of *The New Flora and Silva* magazine.

1

2

3

There is a wildness at the heart of all three of these plants, which makes this a combination to use in areas of the garden set away from more controlled effects around the house. The shrubby rubus sends up fresh light brown stems from the base each season – a useful habit, as it means that by pruning out old growth, you can keep the whole thing to a manageable size. By pruning too, you encourage the shrub to produce the fresh growth that will flower most profusely each year. Pale brown stems arch up and out, bearing three-cornered leaves like those of a blackcurrant bush. In late spring, charming white flowers (like wild roses but without the prickles) are produced all along the stems, weighing them down in graceful arcs. Prune as soon as the flowers have finished. If this rubus bore fruit as well as flowers, it would be perfect, but the flowers are sterile. They are scented though, as, of course, is lily-of-the-valley (*Convallaria*), which you can plant in swathes under the shrub's wide canopy. There will be plenty of room for brunnera too, either the silvered 'Jack Frost' or, if you want a more genuinely wild look, plain-leaved *Brunnera macrophylla*.

Rubus 'Benenden' + *Convallaria majalis* / *Brunnera macrophylla* 'Jack Frost'

(1) *Rubus* 'Benenden'

HEIGHT: 3 m (10 ft)

SPREAD: 3 m (10 ft)

FLOWERING TIME: Late spring

STAR QUALITIES: Retains the soul of a wild, free-spirited thing, enthusiastic and vigorous. Charming flowers, purest white, each with a central boss of yellow stamens. Useful as the centrepiece of a wild corner in the garden.

ALTERNATIVES: *R. biflorus* has chalky-looking young shoots, attractive in winter, but it has unfriendly prickles among its white flowers.

(2) *Convallaria majalis* (Lily-of-the-valley)

Lily-of-the-valley is an old garden favourite that grows from a branched, creeping, horizontal rhizome. It hates being disturbed and is slow to settle when first planted. Where it is happy, it spreads rapidly, and the fresh green leaves are quite strong enough to keep out weeds. The variety 'Géant de Fortin' has larger flowers than ordinary lily-of-the valley, broader foliage, and the useful tendency to flower a week or ten days later. Plant both to extend the season. They also make superb cut flowers as the scent fills a room.

(3) *Brunnera macrophylla* 'Jack Frost'

A hearty plant, verging on the coarse, but very generous with its sprays of forget-me-not blue flowers. These last from mid-spring to early summer, but this variety has handsome silvered leaves, with margins and veins marked out in plain green. These are a great bonus through the rest of the summer and autumn. Coming as it does from Siberia, brunnera is absolutely hardy and trouble-free. A clump will spread to about 60 cm (24 in) with flowering stems 45 cm (18 in) tall.

1

2

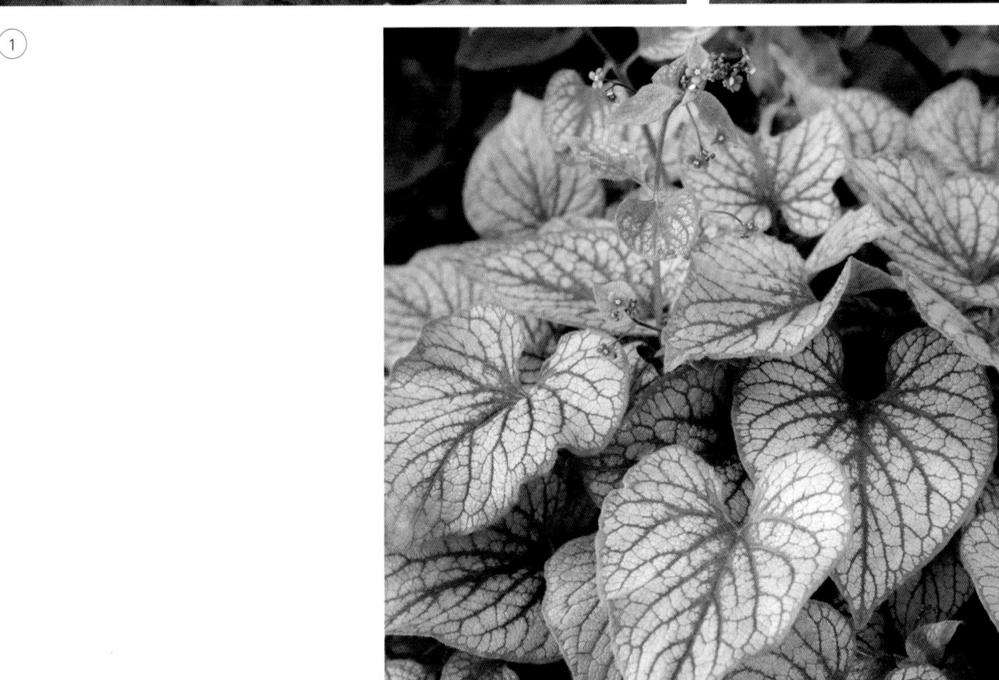

3

Smyrnium is not seen in gardens as often as it deserves to be, given its strange and memorable charm. It is essentially wild at heart and has decided views on where it wants to be. Some gardeners find that scattering very fresh seed direct on the ground is the only way to get it to grow. Others say, equally emphatically, that you must start with good plants, and set them in moist but well-drained soil. It is biennial, so the flowers come in the second year. After flowering, you have to depend on the plant's own self-seeding mechanism for a fresh supply of plants. In the wild, forget-me-nots (*Myosotis*) enjoy the same kind of conditions as the smyrnium, so they make natural companions. But the forget-me-nots must be tall and rangy enough to spread themselves comfortably through the mix. The dwarfed, congested types favoured by breeders will not work here. The only permanent element in this predominately naturalized planting is provided by the iris. The tall stems, which are beginning to show before winter ends, are followed by light-limbed, white fleur-de-lys.

Smyrnium perfoliatum + *Iris orientalis* / *Myosotis sylvatica*

① *Smyrnium perfoliatum*

HEIGHT: 60–120 cm (2–5 ft)

SPREAD: 60 cm (24 in)

FLOWERING TIME: Late spring to early summer

STAR QUALITIES: Perfoliate leaves clasp the stem in an engaging way. Light, airy flower heads have the same luminous green-yellow quality as a spurge.

ALTERNATIVES: *S. olusatrum,* commonly called Alexanders, has larger, more rounded flower heads, but of a much less arresting colour.

② *Iris orientalis*

New foliage is already well above ground in mid-winter and eventually grows to as much as 1.2 m (4 ft). As a foliage plant alone, particularly in a shifting, transient mix such as this, the iris earns its keep, for the sword leaves act as fixed landmarks among the more ephemeral smyrnium and myosotis. The lightly held flowers are white with yellow throats, charming and as wild-looking as their companions.

③ *Myosotis sylvatica* (Forget-me-not)

Seed breeders seem determined to turn forget-me-nots into dwarfs, but for this grouping, avoid any types with 'Ball' or 'Mini' in their names and choose instead a cultivar that, like the wild forget-me-not, reaches 25 cm (10 in). By nature, forget-me-nots are biennials, growing from seed in one season to flower the next. Plants self-seed profusely and make themselves as permanent as any perennial, so you should not need to sow again.

2

1

3

You have to make the most of glorious, late-flowering *Tulipa sprengeri*, because it is the last tulip you will see until the following spring. It opens from an oval bud to a starry red flower with narrow, pointed petals, the colour clear rather than brilliant. The backs of the outer petals are captivatingly washed over with buff suffused with olive and green. *T. sprengeri* increases from seed quite readily, sometimes flourishing in surprisingly shady positions under shrubs. Because tulips put themselves so completely away when they have finished flowering, they need a more permanent companion, but one that will enjoy the same sharply drained position. The ground contained by a retaining wall would be ideal. Here you can create a gravel bed with rosemary, either standing vertically, as with 'Miss Jessopp's Upright', or sprawling over the edge of the wall, which will be the preferred habit of *Salvia rosmarinus* 'Severn Sea'. The Pasque flower (*Pulsatilla*) has beautiful bell-shaped flowers in clear purple, followed by long-lasting fluffy seed heads. The foliage is deeply dissected.

Tulipa sprengeri + *Pulsatilla vulgaris* / *Salvia rosmarinus* 'Miss Jessopp's Upright'

① *Tulipa sprengeri*

HEIGHT: 50 cm (20 in)

SPREAD: 7 cm (3 in)

FLOWERING TIME: Late spring to early summer

STAR QUALITIES: Clear red flower standing bolt upright on its stem.

ALTERNATIVES: No other tulip flowers so late, but other beautiful tulip species are 'Lilac Wonder', selected from *T. saxatilis* Bakeri Group (flowers in early spring) and *T. orphanidea* Whittallii Group (see p.74), a most perfectly formed little tulip of a burnt orange caramel colour. To achieve a natural look, avoid the big garden tulips and stick to the small species.

② *Pulsatilla vulgaris* (Pasque flower)

This is a native of mountain meadows in Europe, emerging in spring with fine, deeply dissected ferny foliage. Later, handsome, bell-shaped flowers rise well above the leaves, nodding on stems covered with silky hairs. The wild flower is usually soft mauve-purple, but strains have been selected with both white and reddish flowers. The blooms are followed by attractive, silky seed heads. Pasque flowers hate winter wet and need well-drained soil in full sun.

③ *Salvia rosmarinus* 'Miss Jessopp's Upright'

The soothing smell of rosemary, is, on its own, sufficient reason to have it in the garden. Grow your own aromatherapy, throw rosemary on a barbecue, put a sprig in your bath or use it to make a herbal tea. Its evergreen foliage, greyish-green, is a great anchor in the garden, especially in winter. Although it is a Mediterranean native, it is reasonably hardy, provided it has its feet in well-drained soil. The main crop of small, pale blue flowers is produced in spring, but the shrub will flower sporadically through the summer.

2

3

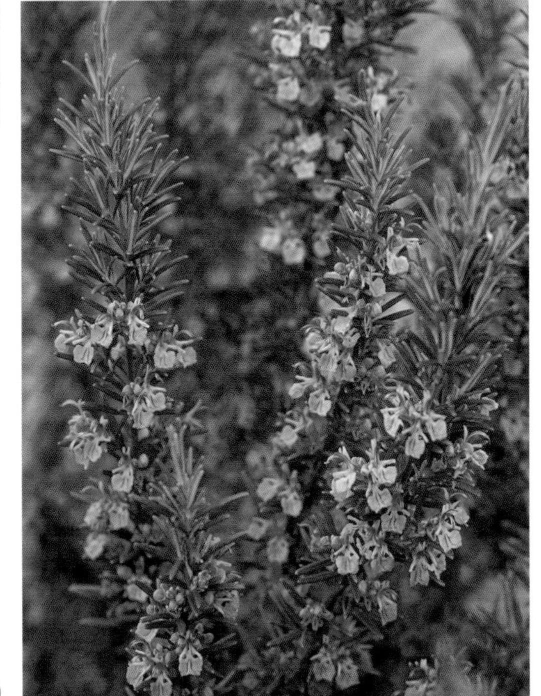

Like many of life's enduring pleasures, violas do not grab you instantly by the throat. Operating little more than 15 cm (6 in) off the ground, they are not built to be grabbers. Instead, they quietly creep up on you, enmeshing you without you realizing what is going on. At this moment in the gardening year, it is possible that nothing in your garden will give you more pleasure than mats of different violas. The flowers sit like well-drilled miniature rent-a-crowds, all gazing in the same direction, each bloom well-mannered enough not to get in the way of the one behind. They might be watching the Queen go by, a few rubber-neckers on each plant craning round the edge of the group to get a better view. Violas, being old-fashioned things, would never bother to line up for a flash in the pan like Madonna. Though small, they are tenacious. All you have to do is deadhead them occasionally, a job to fit in as you wander round your garden in the evening, a glass of wine in hand. The crocus will extend the flowering season of this group back into early spring. The aquilegia will partner the viola.

Viola 'Ardross Gem' + *Aquilegia longissima* / *Crocus tommasinianus* 'Barr's Purple'

(1) *Viola* 'Ardross Gem'

HEIGHT: 15 cm (6 in)

SPREAD: 30 cm (12 in)

FLOWERING TIME: Late spring to late summer

STAR QUALITIES: Wonderful colours of rich mauve-blue, splashed with yellow on the chin. The blue is clearer and brighter than that of most violas. Scented.

ALTERNATIVES: 'Aspasia' is creamy yellow on top, richer yellow below; 'Maggie Mott' is silvery mauve; 'Molly Sanderson' has black petals with the sheen of dangerously expensive satin.

(2) *Aquilegia longissima*

This beautiful aquilegia grows wild on the prairies of southern Arizona and western Texas. Mounds of ferny foliage are topped by soft yellow spurred flowers, delicately scented. It is not as long-lived in the garden as the common granny's bonnet, but it is easy to raise from seed and, where happy, will self-seed. The flowering stems are at least 60 cm (24 in) high. Cut them down after the seed has been shed.

(3) *Crocus tommasinianus* 'Barr's Purple'

The furled buds of *C. tommasinianus* open out flat in the sun to show off their brilliant orange stigmas. 'Barr's Purple', like the similar 'Whitewell Purple', is a richer, deeper colour than the standard species. It is often flowering by late winter, clumps up rapidly and is altogether a paragon.

1

2

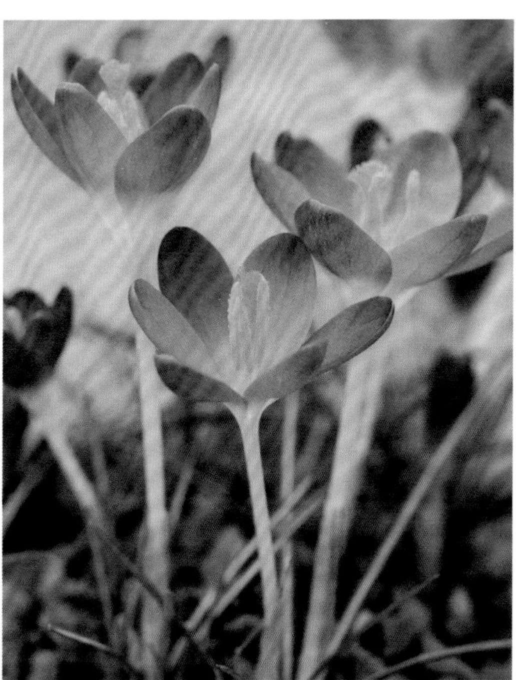

3

For an exuberant planting in the wild style, use this bold trio in damp, boggy soil. The edge of a pool would be ideal. The arum lily (*Zantedeschia*) is borderline hardy, but 'Crowborough', discovered in a Sussex garden, is hardier than most and more tolerant of dry soils. This is a group that needs space, for all three plants have excellent foliage, and they need to look comfortable and relaxed, as natural as they might in their native habitats. Even when the arum's fabulous white spathes, each guarding a yellow poker spadix, have finished, the vast, glossy leaves will continue to please. All three plants in this group hold themselves beautifully, the deeply cut leaves of the ligularia contrasting with the smooth-edged arrows of the arum. Between and around them, you can set the tall sword leaves of the iris, a foil for both the other plants. You scarcely need flowers with leaves as good as these, but the iris's yellow flags should coincide with the ligularia, both following on from the arum.

Zantedeschia aethiopica 'Crowborough' + *Iris pseudacorus* / *Ligularia przewalskii*

① *Zantedeschia aethiopica* 'Crowborough' (Arum lily)

HEIGHT: 90 cm (36 in)

SPREAD: 60 cm (24 in)

FLOWERING TIME: Late spring to mid-summer

STAR QUALITIES: Dramatic white spathes, waxy in texture. Handsome arrow-shaped foliage.

ALTERNATIVES: 'Green Goddess' has spathes tipped and tinged with green; 'Glencoe', also with green-flushed flowers, flowers intermittently from late spring to early autumn.

② *Iris pseudacorus* (Yellow flag iris)

A vigorous iris, with pale green leaves at least 90 cm (36 in) long. It enjoys damp soil, and in the wild grows at the margins of ponds and streams. The yellow flowers appear in mid-summer, several to a stem, and come out in succession. There is a handsome variegated form, 'Variegata' (see p.78), with cream-striped foliage.

③ *Ligularia przewalskii*

Excellent foliage, deeply cut, dark green and held on stems that are nearly black. The flowering stems, also black, rise up above the mounds of leaves to make tall yellow spires, which last from mid- to late summer. The stems will easily reach 2 m (6 ft), and the clumps spread boldly on damp soil to make important landmarks in a garden.

3

2

A brilliant combination of plants with the spires of the white lupin 'Noble Maiden' and the purple and white 'The Governor' holding the stage in front of a shower of blossom from *Deutzia × hybrida* 'Strawberry Fields'.

III

High Summer

A garden in high summer should be awash with flowers and scent, for it is the peak of the gardening year. In uncertain spring and frost-prone autumn, we have to depend on hardy perennials that can withstand sudden plunges in temperature. In summer, we can spread sheets of annual flowers in the garden to grow, flower and set seed within the one breathless season. We can bring succulents and other tender plants out from the greenhouse to take their place in the summer parade. We can plant out temporary exotics among tougher and more permanent plants, where they sit, slightly sniffy, like film stars working in locations much less glamorous than they are themselves. These temporary plantings shift a garden into a different, more colourful gear. It is the garden's equivalent of beachwear.

Gardens, however small, are usually furnished with a few biggish things that mostly stay where they have been put: spurges, perhaps, or the fleshy, arrow-shaped leaves of arum, fat clumps of monkshood and sea holly. Among those set pieces you can use different annuals each year, changing the way the whole area looks. If you have a bitty patch of planting that does not quite hang together, a swathe of cow-parsleyish ammi or orlaya, weaving in and out of the disparate elements in the group, may be just the way to make it sing. If you lose perennial plants or shrubs during winter, then a sowing of annuals such as California poppies or marigolds will fill the bare space beautifully, while you decide whether or not to replace the corpses. Perhaps you will be so enchanted by the gaiety of annual flowers that you will never go back to the Michaelmas daisies or the viburnum. Annuals are not programmed to do anything but flower; their only imperative is to set seed before the summer ends. Then they die. Hardy annuals, such as the California poppy, self-seed easily in soil that is light, open and well-drained. The seed usually germinates in autumn, and the plants survive through winter to flower in early summer.

Unlike most annuals, California poppies (see p.120) have beautiful foliage – grey, finely cut, mounding up in a way that is far more elegant than some grey-leaved perennials such as artemisia. The poorer the soil, the happier they seem to be. They grow beautifully, for instance, in quite fine gravel areas that you might have planted with small species tulips and fritillaries for a spring display. When the bulbs are ending, the California poppies are accelerating into growth again, so they make good partners. The wild kind are brilliant orange, but breeders have developed flowers in cream, pink and mauve, frilly doubles as well as the simpler singles. The Thai Silk series includes a superb range of colours, from pale 'Pink Champagne' to darker, ruffled 'Strawberry Fields'. 'Carmine King' is a deep pink variety known since the 1930s, but it has never gone out of favour. If you cut stems in the morning before the buds unfurl, the flowers of California poppies will last several days inside.

It is difficult to make an ugly eschscholzia, as they are properly called. Sow them among tulips to take over when the bulbs have finished flowering. You could do the same among bearded irises, but the California poppy looks equally good mixed with other annuals, built on its own light, airy lines. Try it with the annual greater quaking grass, *Briza maxima*. Although eschscholzias self-seed readily, the flowers gradually drift away from the posh semi-doubles in exotic shades, settling into the plain but still lovely bright orange blooms they produce in the wild. Small children can spend a productive hour easing off the pointed dunce cap bud cases to release the tightly packed silk chiffon inside. Give them full sun, and don't forget that they thrive in poor soil. Most annuals can be raised from seed in pots (you get much better plants this way), but California poppies have carrot-like roots, not easy to transplant successfully, so are best sown direct into the ground. There are three things to remember. First, do not sow too soon. If the soil is still cold and wet, the seed will rot. Second, rake and smooth the soil to make a welcoming bed. A small seed cannot break its way through hefty clods of clay. Third, sow thinly.

Hardy annuals are best sown from mid-spring onwards, but some half-hardy annuals can be started earlier in pots under cover. The difference between the two is that seedlings of hardy annuals can usually stagger through winter. Seedlings of half-hardies (snapdragons, cleomes, cosmos, tobacco plants, French marigolds, zinnias) cannot. None of these can be planted outside until the danger of frosty nights has passed. Half-hardy annuals are superb additions to a flower garden and great for cutting too. Given mild weather, spider flowers (*Cleome*) can still look good in late autumn. The white kind, 'Helen Campbell', is particularly lovely. Plants take a long time (minimum eighteen weeks) to work up to flowering size, so you need to give them an early start. Cleomes bear big, rounded heads of flower with weird spider legs sticking out. They make robust plants (1.2 m / 4 ft tall), more like perennials than annuals, and look terrific mixed with the ever-useful *Verbena bonariensis* (see p.180) or set against mounds of evergreen *Euphorbia characias* (see p.70).

Of course, seed catalogues are full of promises, and it is not the seedsman's role to explain how often seedlings might damp off, or how attached mice are to sweet peas, or how tricky is the escape mechanism that nature has devised for some kinds of seed. Seedsmen depend on a gardener's perennial optimism, and they are right. Despite crushing autumns, wallowing winters, gales, floods and the impression, at winter's end, that one has been living in a cave for a very long time, it is right that we are seduced by bright images of daisy-flowered rudbeckias and airy love-in-a-mist (*Nigella*).

Nigella, like the California poppy, has excellent foliage – thread-like, airy, creating a pale cloud of green around the blue flowers. You can use it to great effect between bearded irises, because it does not shade their rhizomes (which they hate), and in those crowded spaces, where it might be difficult for you to intrude, it will seed itself, giving a slightly different effect each season. The standard variety is *Nigella damascena* 'Miss Jekyll' (p.146). *N. hispanica* is more interesting, with black-centred flowers pierced by startling maroon-red stamens. The blue of the petals is deeper than 'Miss Jekyll', and the patterning of the flowers is more intricate. It makes the same kind of filigree foliage (though darker) as *N. damascena*, and the seed pods are extravagantly wonderful, curving from an urn shape into eight-horned tips. The plants shed their seed from late summer onwards; these self-seeded plants are, of course, the earliest into flower the following season. Each spring, you can add fresh seed of one kind or another to give a later flush of flowers. In time, these self-seeding annuals will make a self-sustaining colony, and their randomness gives a pleasing, relaxed air to the garden. They are putting themselves where they want to be, and we can learn from that as our gardens become more natural.

That easy, natural look is enhanced by using annuals that are themselves wild species, such as the bishop's flower, *Ammi majus*, its close cousin *Visnaga daucoides* (formerly *Ammi visnaga*, p.144) and the white lace flower *(Orlaya grandiflora*; see p.64). Both have a boho, slightly wild look that works as well in a vase as it does in the garden. Like the best kind of aunt, ammi is at home in any company. If you sow in late summer, by autumn you will have fine, fat plants to set out together with lilies and tulips. This way, you can get three flowerings from the same patch of ground, with the ammi filling in the months between the spring tulips and the lilies of high summer.

You can sow orlaya at the same time and in the same way, and by late autumn you will have well-rooted plants to put into the ground. Autumn-sown plants tend to grow more robustly than spring ones. At 60 cm (24 in), orlaya is shorter than ammi (1 m / 3 ft), so you need to use it further forward in a border. The white flower heads are differently made, flattish still but with several big, pouting petals arranged among the froth of smaller ones. From a spring sowing, you can expect flowers after three months, and they will look good for the next two months outside. You can use them as cut flowers too, though they will not last more than a week or so in a vase. But seed is cheap, and the flowers are easy to grow. Sow a row of ammi or orlaya among the vegetables, and use those for cutting to avoid robbing the garden.

Annuals that have good foliage (like love-in-a-mist and California poppies) are a huge asset in the summer garden, billowing quietly to fill space between more heavily built perennials and shrubs. Ammi is similarly endowed, producing a foamy mass of dull green, very finely cut. You get bulk, but with finesse. Over this appears wave after wave of flat white flower heads, 11–12 cm (4 in) across, made up, like cow parsley, of masses of individual flowers. Insects love them. Each stem produces thirty or more heads, and they take it in turns to perform over a long time. You could have ammi collapsing into the woody stems of a spice-flavoured pelargonium, ammi mixing with the second flowering of giant chives, ammi with cornflowers or equally happy with the more purplish blue of stokesia, ammi with the now dulled heads of cerinthe.

Altogether too much ammi, you might feel. But it is an easy, casual guest in the garden, welcome wherever it goes. Unstaked, it flops onto its elbows, but sometimes this is an advantage, as along a path, where it can thread itself through chives, pinks, violas and late alliums such as *A. angulosum*. Because it is so airy, it never smothers them. *Ammi majus* comes from the Mediterranean – southern Europe, Turkey, North Africa – which gives you an idea of the kind of summers it is hoping for. The Fibonacci marvel that is *Visnaga daucoides* (p.144) is native to North Africa, particularly Egypt, Morocco and Tunisia. In some respects, it is even better than its cousin, *Ammi majus*

– the foliage is much more feathery, as good as fennel. It makes a taller, bulkier plant, and the flower heads are more densely constructed, the baby florets packed tightly into elegant domes. It is not showy – the flower heads are a soft greenish-white – but it is a superb filler, airily elegant beside, for instance, the chunkier, meatier strap foliage of agapanthus, which will often be flowering with it. Structurally, it is a strong plant, and the flat flower heads, bleached cream, may stand as skeletal forms right through winter.

Growing Grasses

Planting in the summer garden may encompass a great swathe of grasses – miscanthus, deschampsia, calamagrostis, molinia – which are essential elements of the so-called 'prairie planting' or New Perennial movement, which brought a German and Dutch-inspired style of gardening into Britain and North America to push aside the delphiniums and lupins of the traditional herbaceous border. Grasses are generally seen to best advantage when contrasted with plants that have completely different attributes, whether in terms of foliage, as with acanthus or hostas, or colour, as with annuals such as bold orange tithonia or marigolds. You could use miscanthus behind astrantia, Bowles's golden sedge (*Carex elata* 'Aurea') with some big, green-leaved hosta and perhaps a foreground of the bronze-leaved celandine 'Brazen Hussey'. The foxy red and copper-toned leaves of *Carex buchananii* associate well with a whipcord hebe. You can use them too, to take over where spring-flowering bulbs have finished, using *Calamagrostis × acutiflora* 'Karl Foerster' (see p.58) to follow camassias and alliums, or miscanthus to fill a space where the dark tulip 'Negrita' and the beautiful lily-flowered 'Ballerina' once bloomed. Allow the bronze-purple heads of *Pennisetum alopecuroides* 'Hameln' to wave between clumps of alchemilla. Annual grasses such as the quaking grass, *Briza maxima*, make enchanting companions for pinks and violas. *B. maxima* has very good seed heads, like small woven lockets, which tremble on threadlike stems. White hare's tail (*Lagurus ovatus*; p.130) has shorter, furry heads, especially soft and graceful. These annual varieties are fairly short, between 45 and 60 cm (18 to 24 in) high, useful to plug gaps in foreground plantings and easy to raise from seed.

The flowering stems of some of the taller grasses can reach 1.5 m (5 ft) in a season, arching like fountains. These types look best planted so that they do not get too closely muddled with their neighbours. Nothing we can do for them will make them more beautiful than they are themselves, though we can give them decent neighbours: lots of sedums, echinaceas and astrantias. The great advantage of the grasses is that they continue to contribute long after most flowering perennials have dived underground. Leaves and seed heads fade to shades of buff and cream, but the shapes can stay looking good until the end of the year. Wind and rain are the enemies. (So are their names. *Pennisetum alopecuroides* 'Hameln' feels as uncomfortable in the mouth as a half-chewed dictionary. Ferns suffer from the same problem.)

Stipa tenuissima, an upright, densely tufted grass, has become a favourite not so much for its bright green, fading to buff foliage as for its tactile beauty. Of all grasses, it is the one that almost unconsciously we reach out to touch. Our fingers run through it easily, and it feels as delightful as trailing one's hand through water. Jolly companions such as nasturtiums are what it needs to enliven its stonewashed tones. If unmolested by caterpillars, nasturtiums will put on a double show, the flowers of high summer followed by another crop in early autumn. In dampish, well-fed ground they produce a lot of foliage – some would say too much – but their fleshy abundance is a wonderfully generous antidote to the rather pinched appearance of the stipa. The peppery tang their leaves give to a salad is welcome too. The variegated kinds of nasturtium are too busy, too hectic, but 'Empress of India' (see p.124) is superb – dark, velvet flowers amid lustrous dark foliage. Much of the seed the plants produce is hidden away in the winter larders of rodents, but each year some self-seeded plants will appear. You can add to the mix each season: perhaps some cream and apricot flowers to add to the hotter reds and oranges that nasturtiums, left to themselves, will produce. A smattering of the dark-leaved varieties such as 'Empress of India' or 'Princess of India' is also a bonus. Some nasturtiums clump, while others creep. If you want to cover the space between the *Stipa tenuissima* as quickly as possible, then the creeping ones should be your first choice.

Equally brilliant interspersed with the stipa would be a dancing troupe of Mexican zinnias. Zinnias

Top: An exuberant display of orange California poppies (*Eschscholzia californica*) fronts a summer border, with campanulas adding cooler tones behind.

Above: The white plumes of *Calamagrostis brachytricha* make a smoky backdrop for yellow daisy-flowered *Rudbeckia fulgida* var. *deamii* and mauve mounds of *Aster × frikartii* 'Jungfrau'. Grey-leaved *Anaphalis triplinervis* 'Sommerschnee' fills in the foreground of a border at Foggy Bottom, Bressingham Gardens, Diss, Norfolk, UK.

are such outrageous flowers that we assume they must be difficult to grow. They are not: seed germinates generously within four days, and once started into growth, they zoom helter-skelter onwards. But they also hate frost and cannot be planted out until late spring or early summer. If you do not want the bother of growing from seed, buy small plants and grow them on. Grow plenty: they make superb cut flowers.

The big, bushy zinnia plants come into flower in high summer. They will still be flowering in autumn and are fabulous enough to upstage even a dahlia, despite being only a tenth of its size. Some varieties produce vast footballs of flowers in shocking pink, orange and yellow, some are an extraordinary chartreuse green, and some have wonderfully complex centres, the stamens ringed in contrasting colours. Few are boring. By nature, zinnias make wonderfully muscular, meaty growth on strong stems that do not need support. Don't miss the ice-green variety 'Envy', which is gorgeous – 50 cm (20 in) high with lime-green flowers. 'Mazurkia' has scarlet flowers tipped with cream. 'Scabious Flowered' has huge, crested flowers in a mixture of scarlet, carmine, pink, yellow, orange and cream.

The first zinnia to arrive in this country was *Z. pauciflora*. Its name ('few flowers') suggests that it was an unimpressive performer, and Philip Miller, who grew it at the Chelsea Physic Garden in London in the 1750s, was not enthusiastic. Most of today's garden varieties have been bred from another Mexican species, *Z. elegans*. This was growing in Britain by 1796 thanks to the Marchioness of Bute, wife of the Ambassador to the Spanish court. She was given it by Professor Ortega of Madrid, who also supplied her with the first dahlias seen in Britain.

Alongside drifts of taller grasses, such as *Deschampsia cespitosa* 'Goldschleier', try perennials such as dark-leaved *Anthriscus sylvestris* 'Ravenswing', some big groups of Spuria iris (as much for their fine, tall foliage as for their flowers), a deep blue monkshood such as *Aconitum* 'Bressingham Spire' (see p.140), angelica, or a Siberian iris such as the fine 'Mountain Lake'. As well as introducing colour into the communities of grasses, look for contrasts in structure, such as the silvery sea holly Miss Willmott's Ghost (*Eryngium giganteum*; see p.132) will provide. The short-lived perennials *Euphorbia oblongata* and *Verbena bonariensis* (see p.180) are also excellent companions. They always grow (and consequently look) better in places where they put themselves than in the carefully prepared billets you prepare for them. To give the grasses company in the spring, add the enchanting, ivory-coloured narcissus 'Petrel', which has several reflexed flowers on each stem.

Prairie planting, as its name implies, works best where there is space for plants to be introduced in big spreads. But you can tinker productively in smaller spaces making your own bit of 'wilderness' with a matrix of *Stipa tenuissima* and bronze carex tying together *Euphorbia cyparissias*, silver-blue eryngium, small yellow stars of tickseed (*Coreopsis*) and occasional giant spires of *Verbascum olympicum*. Or you can go in the opposite direction and instead of trying to create a matrix, use just one fantastic grass, such as *Stipa gigantea* (see p.184), to pour its seed heads into the low light of a late summer afternoon. It grows like a clump of wild oats, rising and spreading its stems in a great arc, particularly beautiful when seen against the light. The stems can be up to 2.5 m (8 ft) tall, purplish-green when they first emerge but bleaching to a soft straw colour as they ripen. It is magnificent. Keep the planting around it simple. Give it just one companion: the Mexican sunflower (*Tithonia rotundifolia* 'Torch'; see p.186). It is tall – anything from 1.2 m (4 ft) upwards – and of an uncompromisingly brilliant orange. Despite its common name, it is not at all like a sunflower; rather, it is more like a single zinnia, each bloom rising from a green sheath that is, as the name suggests, just like a torch holder. The flowers peak in the gap that so often opens up in a garden between July and October. Once it gets going, it flowers non-stop until it gets frosted. The stems are thick and robust, so you don't have to stake. It is a half-hardy annual, easy from seed, though not quick. To impress, as they are eminently capable of doing, tithonias need a hot summer, however, and over that, we have no control.

Quintessential Poppies

Poppies in particular capture the brilliance and fleetingness of summer, a distillation of the summer garden in their bright, fragile petals. They are easy to grow, and they provide an incredibly diverse set of possibilities for a gardener. Shirley poppies, for instance, selected from the wild Flanders or corn poppy (*Papaver rhoeas*), can be pink, orange, red, white or smudgy-mauve, double or single. All are enchanting. The name sounds as if it might have come from some Shirley Templesque girl, given to floating chiffon, but not so. The flowers are the creation of the Reverend William Wilks, one of those fortunate nineteenth-century English clergymen whose gardening took precedence in their lives. Wilks was vicar in the village of Shirley, near Croydon (now in south London), and created the strain from a single white-edged poppy growing among the wild, plain red ones in a corner of his vicarage garden. Wilks marked the flower, and the following year he raised 200 plants from the single seed head. He thinned out his plants severely, and for twenty years selected only the best of the seedlings to grow on. In this laborious way, he created a strain of poppies in a wide range of colours that look like tissue paper left out in the rain. 'I am about my flowers between three and four o'clock in the morning', he wrote, 'so as to pull up and trample on the bad ones before the bees have a chance of conveying pollen to others.'

There are many excellent seed strains of *P. rhoeas*, including 'Angel's Choir', which produces fragile, double-flowered Shirley poppies in fabulous bruised colours: dirty greyish-pink, Victorian dove mauve, some colours with a picotee edge of a paler colour round their petals. By selecting and saving seed from flowers with the colours you like best, you can continue to fine-tune a seed mixture to your own ends, abandoning the colours you do not like and strengthening the shades you want. This is how breeders came up with the variety *P.* 'Amazing Grey', a Shirley poppy with papery petals in more shades of misty, shimmering grey than you ever knew existed. Scatter seed direct in a sunny place, perhaps between clumps of fountain grass, such as *Pennisetum alopecuroides* 'Hameln' or 'Red Head'. Use them to extend the season after early summer bulbs such as *Triteleia laxa* 'Corrina' have finished flowering. Grow them with equally sun-loving companions such as thyme and grey-leaved pinks (*Dianthus*). The grey-tinged selections of the Shirley poppy look especially wonderful surrounded by the silvery-grey tones of dianthus foliage.

Opium poppies, varieties of *Papaver somniferum* (see p.64), will be looking for different companions. They want a different soil too, something heavier and damper than would suit the Shirley poppies. Where they are happy, plants will grow 90 cm (36 in) tall, with masses of buds. The leaves are handsome, the best of all the poppies – rich, waxy, silvery. The common kind has purple flowers with dark smudges at the bottoms of the petals, which are ranged around a ring of pale cream stamens. Bumblebees come stumbling out of the flowers covered in white pollen. But other colours crop up too – look for a fine, deep plum-purple variety called 'Lauren's Grape', a beautiful magenta with purple smudges, or a rich red. The seedlings of good forms often have leaves that are more intricately edged (as if they have been cut with pinking shears) than the ordinary kinds. The flowers do not last long, but the round seed heads are dramatic and persist on strong stems before being shredded by a little beetle that loves to eat the seeds. When the foliage starts to get drab and scrappy, you can pull up the opium poppies that you do not want, leaving the best ones to self-seed.

Some of the opium poppies make great powderpuff flowers, especially doubles such as pink 'Candy Floss' or the dramatic 'Black Beauty'. Use opium poppies among delphiniums or between stems of dark *Angelica gigas* (see p.136). They are also good with eryngiums and thalictrums, catmint and penstemons. They will seed themselves in places where you might never have thought of putting them, often in combinations more pleasing than the ones you planned yourself. Self-seeding is always to be encouraged, and it is one of the huge advantages of growing annual flowers. It confers a sense of abundance and brings about a certain ambience in a garden: relaxed, tranquil, laid-back, in which our relationship with plants becomes a partnership of equals.

Thinking about Colour

Views on colour are one of the most instantly articulated expressions of taste. We register colour and have views on it more quickly and more certainly than on any other aspect of our surroundings. But the thing about gardens is that they shift all the time. For a short spell, a poppy border may well be an all-red border, but when the poppies are finished, the border can shift into a completely different gear, perhaps majoring in tall tobacco plants in cool lime-green and white.

Single-colour borders that stick to one colour throughout the year seem to be an easy option, promising a way of avoiding difficult decisions about what goes with what – but they are much more difficult to do well than mixed borders. A blue flower does not necessarily go with another flower that is also blue. It may look much better against a white flower or a yellow one. This is true, for instance, of the veronica called 'Crater Lake Blue' and *Campanula latifolia*. Both are blue, but the veronica is an intense, brilliant, true blue, while the campanula is a drifty, mauveish, much more recessive blue. Together they look awful. The veronica, being a clean, straight colour, can take another clean colour nearby – white moon daisies or the clear yellow of the corn marigold (*Glebionis segetum*). The campanula sings in a minor key and needs other non-primary colours with it: dirty pink astrantias, deep purplish clematis, lime-green tobacco flowers.

White is one of the most difficult colours to handle effectively. Vita Sackville-West made it look dangerously easy at Sissinghurst, Kent, the garden she started to make in the 1930s, but the dead chalk white of a plant such as sweet rocket is hideous next to the much creamier white of a rose such as 'Nevada'. In a garden setting, the creamy whites are much more easy-going than dead whites. They do not draw the eye so insistently and are accommodating neighbours. The dead whites can often be used only in a single mass, set perhaps against a dark green hedge, with little else in view. The white of sweet rocket is a stark, harsh white, and these straight colours are harder to place properly than oblique ones such as white foxgloves, which are actually slightly creamy, slightly greeny. The Edwardian gardener Gertrude Jekyll preached that white flowers should be set off by touches of blue or lemon-yellow, a gospel followed in the 1930s by the great gardener Phyllis Reiss at Tintinhull in Somerset, where the white flowers in the Fountain Garden were thrown into relief against grey-blue and acid yellow.

The American gardener Lawrence Johnston, who acquired Hidcote in Gloucestershire in 1907, made a similarly subtle 'white' garden. He did not choose a dead white rose to fill the beds there but *Rosa* 'Gruss an Aachen', which has creamy flowers overlaid with soft pink. The white osteospermums and the white tobacco plants used in the garden are also both slightly off-white, the one overlaid with blue, the other with green. The pale colours glow there against the dark backdrop of clipped yew and box. White gardens are infinitely more effective in shade than in sun.

But how limiting single-colour gardens are! If you have masses of space, then it is no hardship to set aside a corner for a white garden or a swathe of wall for a blue border. Few gardeners have that kind of space, however. They want different parts of the garden to feel different, and single-colour groupings cut out too many options and often fail to make plants sing as well as they should. The white flowered *Lilium regale* (p.144), for instance, is a brilliant plant, the flowers held in elegant trumpets round the stem. But if you put this cool beauty in front of a white-flowered campanula in a regulation white display, the two things just melt into each other. On the other hand, if you try the same plant in a mixed group with the variegated foliage of the phlox 'Norah Leigh', the dark-leaved euphorbia 'Chameleon' and (at a safe distance) the anchusa 'Loddon Royalist', you get a far richer and better effect. You could add spires of the verbascum 'Gainsborough' to come into lemon-yellow flower when the spurge finishes. That might set your heart beating faster than any white garden ever has, even Vita Sackville-West's.

The purple border at Sissinghurst is more interesting than the white, because it encompasses every colour from red through to deep blue. In autumn, the scarlet hips of the 'Geranium' rose (a hybrid from *Rosa moyesii*) are the best things in the border, adding great punches of vitality into what otherwise could be quite a heavy scheme. Earlier in the year there are wine-purple alliums, magenta geraniums, deep blue salvias and pale *Clematis* 'Perle d'Azur' with irises and asters, penstemons and a touch – not too much – of purple foliage from the smoke bush, *Cotinus coggygria* 'Foliis Purpureis'. It is an imposing scheme, operatic and high-octane, but not one that is necessarily easy to live with. Dark, rich tones, such as you get in the leaves of *Hylotelephium telephium* 'Mohrchen' (where they have a metallic sheen), are less oppressive if they are leavened with paler colours. The hylotelephium (sedum), for instance, looks excellent with the pale striped foliage of *Sisyrinchium striatum* 'Aunt May' and the capricious spurred flowers of a columbine such as *Aquilegia longissima* (see p.94).

Thinking only of colour can blind you to the rest of a plant's attributes, and its faults. Flowers are only one of the tricks that a plant can perform, and it is a shorter act than foliage or form. If you garden with

Top: *Hedychium* 'Tara' adds a tropical touch to one of Graham Gough's exuberant combinations in the garden at Marchants, near Lewes in Sussex, UK. Packed in beside the ginger are *Agapanthus caulescens*, *Symphyotrichum* 'Marchants Early Purple' and the delicate flowers of *Oenothera lindheimeri*.

Above: In the south garden at Morton Hall, Holberrow Green, Worcestershire, UK, misty blue stems of Russian sage (*Salvia yangii*) rise up alongside *Sidalcea* 'Elsie Heugh', *Agapanthus* 'Blue Triumphator' and tobacco flowers (*Nicotiana* 'Lime Green').

single-colour borders, you are much more likely to swoop on a plant because it is blue or white or yellow and overlook the fact that its leaves are as inviting as last week's salad and that it holds itself with all the grace of a sailor on a spree. Whether colours 'go' will always depend on personal taste. A clamorous border of oriental poppies might be too strong an effect for many gardeners, but the poppies are all on the same side of the line that divides orange-reds from blue-reds. Magenta *Gladiolus communis* subsp. *byzantinus* (see p.134) is on the other side of the divide and looks spectacularly bad with the poppies.

The colour of a particular plant can be used to reinforce the lines of a design – or to knit together areas of a garden that are unsatisfactory because of a bad design. Used this way, the colour is more likely to come from foliage than flower. The golden leaves of a hosta can act subtly as a series of signposts through a garden. So can the dark foliage of the herbaceous *Clematis recta* 'Purpurea' or bronze-leaved fennel. Even in high summer, you still need mounds of foliage to set off your flowers; it is the velvet on which the crown jewels are displayed.

Foliage Framework

Flowers need foliage. The dictum ought to be scratched into the concrete of every patio, emblazoned on every garden gate, carved on the handle of every garden spade. An obsession with colour has been the distinguishing characteristic of many gardeners who were brought up to revere Sissinghurst, with its single-colour borders, above all other gardens and to believe that the only true path to the gardener's Nirvana lay through a series of agonized choices about the exact nature of the flowers we put in our patches.

'Darling! Salmon! How brave!' exclaim the white garden brigade as they sharpen their pruning knives for a horticultural mercy killing. You might as well fall on your garden fork there and then as try and explain that the point of the rodgersia they are looking at is not the buff-pink flower but the whorls of bronze leaves underneath it. This obsession with colour and with particular modish flowers has got in the way of a vital tenet of good gardening: leaves are vastly more important in creating satisfying and enduring planting schemes than flowers. A garden that is all flowers is like a cake that is all icing. And in town gardens, set in the midst of concrete, tarmac, noise, dust and general mayhem, you desperately need cool, still oases of green to set off occasional bursts of colour.

When you first start to garden, you are seduced by flowers. You open a catalogue, visit a garden centre and see only the colour of things. You grab plants indiscriminately, favouring the ones that are actually in flower at that moment. But being impressed by a plant because of its flowers is like judging a man entirely on the basis of his Armani jacket. (Unfortunately, some plants, like some people, have little more to offer, and although they may be fine in a crowd, you would not want to spend too much time with them on their own.) Annual flowers are wonderful; they are essential components of a summer garden, but they rarely have impressive leaves and consequently look much better when they can borrow the foliage of other plants than when they are planted on their own. They are the curlicues, the garnishes in a garden, though some fine exceptions, such as ammi and orlaya, have enough beef in them to constitute the main course.

To get a sustaining backbone into a garden, you need plants that look their best for more than a six-week flowering period. When you swoop on a plant in flower at the garden centre, ask yourself, 'What will this look like without its flowers? Will it develop an interesting shape? What are its leaves like?' If you judge a plant by these criteria, flowers become a bonus, rather than the sole *raison d'être*. Some of these key backbone plants should be evergreen, so that in winter the garden does not entirely dissolve into a skein of skeletal branches. This is where shrubs such as daphne, mahonia and myrtle are so useful. The spurge *Euphorbia characias* (see p.70) is also a great ally in this respect, making solid mounds of evergreen foliage spiralling around stout upright stems. Its main season is spring, but even when, after several months, you finally cut down the spent flower heads, the foliage lends its splendid sea-green bulk to any summer flowers you might arrange around it. It always enhances, never detracts.

E. characias, like the hosta, is a foliage plant with a capital F. Other plants, such as crocosmia, are not so firmly labelled, but although you might leap on it because of its arched sprays of brilliant red flowers, you will gradually find that the long, pleated, sword-shaped leaves are of equal consequence. You need these sharp verticals to give variety in plant groups. Use the deep scarlet crocosmia 'Hellfire' (p.124) with the dark-leaved dahlia 'Bishop of Llandaff', which has flowers of an equally outrageous colour. You may have chosen both plants on account of their late summer display, but long before either of them comes into flower in high summer you will have had the pleasure of the contrast in foliage.

Most foliage has bulk; not all has beauty. Sometimes you may be prepared to accept boring leaves for the sake of some other attribute, such as scent. There may be something about the smell of the plant's flowers that makes you suspend judgment on its other qualities. You float on that smell, feeling good about the world and loving your neighbour, and for that you are prepared to let slip a leaf that is no more than leafish. This is not to say that you should have nothing in your garden that you could not defend in front of a foliage tribunal – only that you should have some good reason for including anything that would not stand up in such a court.

Where, as with the crocosmia, you get foliage and flowers of equal value, you are in clover (another double act). These are the plants to favour. Rodgersia is another winner. It is often portrayed as a bog plant but is perfectly happy in ordinary soil, provided it is not a dust bowl. There is not a dud in the whole family. The flowers come out in summer in showy plush plumes of pink or white, but the plants have already paid two months' garden rent with their leaves, which are outstanding. *Rodgersia aesculifolia* has glossy bronze foliage, the leaflets radiating out like the spokes of an umbrella from a central stalk, the end of each leaflet bluntly cut like a horse chestnut leaf. *Rodgersia pinnata* (see p.78) has leaves similarly arranged but without the gloss. The leaflets do not have the same blunt end, and the plant is less massively built. Ferns are natural companions, either the tall shuttlecock fern, *Matteuccia struthiopteris* (see p.142), or the more delicately built maidenhair fern (*Adiantum aleuticum*; see p.174); so is the grass *Pennisetum*, with its caterpillar seed heads.

Playing with Purple

Some foliage needs to be used with a light hand. Purple is the trickiest, because it can give an over-heavy, saturated effect if used in the great wodges that purple berberis or purple nut (*Corylus maxima* 'Purpurea') thrust upon the eye. But purple combines well with equally rich colours such as royal blue and cardinal red to make dramatic planting schemes. What gardener could do without irises, alliums, tulips, hellebores, sweet williams and fritillaries? Purple has found a place even in minimalist gardens, where only spiky things or isolated clumps of plants with green flowers are allowed to sully the clear, swept expanses of concrete and smooth sheets of aluminium. It goes very well with grey, and it has more angst than white.

Alliums, particularly, find favour, because of their dramatic structure as well as their colour. All are built on roughly the same lines, a stem with a blob on top, and most (but not all) are purple. The differences have to do with the proportion of stem to blob. *A. cristophii* is squat and top-heavy, with too much blob for its stem, but has sufficient presence to overcome its inbuilt design problem. *A. sphaerocephalon* has 60 cm (24 in) of stem, which leads you to expect something rather splendid at the top; in fact, the flower is rather small, but it is interestingly pear-shaped. At first it appears green with a cap of purple, but gradually the purple floods through the rest of the flower, until by high summer the whole head is glowing. Use it with opium poppies, whose silver-grey seed heads tone beautifully with purple, and add perhaps a scatter of the annual hare's tail grass, *Lagurus ovatus* (see p.130). *Allium giganteum* is the family's Grand Slam, with huge balls balanced on 1.2 m (4 ft) stems. Even the bulbs are monsters. The extra height is useful in a garden planting: at Hidcote, the National Trust garden in Gloucestershire, these alliums are used down the back of a border of double peonies. They would also make good companions for the supreme foliage plant *Melianthus major*, perhaps with agapanthus to pick up the baton later.

If you love purple, you will not be short of plants with which to try out saturated schemes. Think of violas, lupins and the beautiful dark-leaved angelica, *A. gigas* (see p.136). Think of the gorgeous cow parsley called *Anthriscus sylvestris* 'Ravenswing', with its purplish-brown foliage, or the elegant fountain grass *Pennisetum advena* 'Rubrum', with leaves and flowering heads that look as though they have been soaked in claret. Pastels are fine – drifts of grey, billows of pink, washing-powder white – but this is gardening for sleepwalkers. White appeals to those who like

Top: Branches of the shrubby *Rosa × odorata* 'Mutabilis' hang over a summer border rich with opium poppies (*Papaver somniferum*), *Salvia* 'Amistad' and the variegated foliage of *Miscanthus sinensis* 'Variegatus'.

Above: A summer border at Arabella Lennox-Boyd's garden, Gresgarth Hall, in Lancashire, UK, displays flat heads of sedum, with phlox and blue spikes of agastache, together with sea holly (*Eryngium*) and *Selinum wallichianum*.

everything to be neat and tidy, according to the National Garden Bureau in the United States, which once explored the psychology of colour in gardens. The study had nothing to say about purple. Perhaps it was censored. There is something altogether more dangerous about purple than white.

Pink is good with purple, provided it is the deep, saturated kind. Try the inky aquilegia *A.* 'William Guiness' with sheets of brilliant dianthus in front of it. Try pink bleeding heart, *Lamprocapnos spectabilis*, planted in front of the herbaceous clematis *C. recta* 'Purpurea', which has leaves heavily saturated with purple. Use the dirty purple Oriental poppy *P.* 'Patty's Plum' with sheaves of the magenta-flowered gladiolus, *G. communis* subsp. *byzantinus* (see p.134).

Purple also works with rich royal blues, such as anchusa provides. Hairy anchusa, with its searingly blue flowers, is an unreliable perennial, but when you see well-grown plants, they are not easily forgotten. Use them behind purple bearded irises such as 'Langport Wren' (short) or 'Swazi Princess' (much taller), or combine them with giant alliums. Try deep bronze fennel to fill in the gaps, or perhaps some first-year plants of purple angelica.

Later in the summer season, you could start a purplish group with a plant such as *Verbena bonariensis* (see p.180), which is all stem and no leaf. The thin stems branch in an angular way, and at the end of each branch is a tuft of flowers. They start coming out as high summer begins and are still performing at the onset of winter, their tall, skeletal forms waltzing along with flowers of *Salvia* 'Amistad' (see p.176). Although the verbena is tall, up to 1.5 m (5 ft), it is so wiry and insubstantial that you can see through it easily. Use it like a bead curtain at the front of a border, to provide a tantalizing screen for something that lies beyond. Among the stems of the verbena you could use one of the scrambling purple-magenta geraniums, such as *G.* 'Russell Prichard' or 'Ann Folkard', which would thicken up the mass but not get in the way of the verbena's flowers. Few garden plants have such a long season of flower as 'Russell Prichard': it starts in early summer and continues until autumn, when the long, scrambling side branches die back to the compact, central crown.

Where there is space for it to spread its wide wands of flower, use dierama with the verbena, or instead of it. The tall kind, *Dierama pulcherrimum*, has flowering stems that make great arcs bending away from the central clumps of grassy leaves. The flowers are magenta bells, though they are purple in bud and purple again as they die. The buds emerge from dry, buff paper cases and hang on threads so fine that you cannot see them.

In the garden, purple plants work best when they are set against other colours that throw them into relief. But which colours? Purple does not work with white, because the contrast is harsh and unsympathetic, but it works with cream, with orange (if you are really brave) and, best of all, with its sister colours red, deep pink and blue. Purple-leaved plants often act as the anchor of a group, with more seasonal companions ebbing and flowing around them. Sometimes, as with the superb foliage plant *Rheum palmatum* 'Atrosanguineum', the purples themselves ebb and flow. Rheum is a fancy sort of rhubarb with large, gorgeous, jagged leaves. In spring it is mesmerizing: great clenched fists of buds, glossy and impatient. The flowers shoot up, panicles of purplish-red, towards late spring, then it collapses. Totally. But you can quickly fill the gap with summer purples – cannas such as *C.* 'Roi Humbert', perhaps. Or you could move in a dahlia such as 'Arabian Night', with flowers that are practically black over green foliage. Even better is *D.* 'Grenadier', in which the purple rests in the leaves, and the flowers are a rich, singing red. Neither canna nor dahlia can go out until frosts are a thing of the past, so it is very selfless of the rheum to pack itself away at exactly the right time for new troops to come in.

Plants in the *Artemisia lactiflora* Guizhou Group will give you more permanent summer effects – feathery mounds of well-cut leaves drowned in purple. In late spring, however, you will only have the artemisia's foliage to play with, so you might splash purple tulips round it, such as 'Negrita' or cream and purple 'Shirley'. Later in summer, when the artemisia is enormous – up to 1.5 m (5 ft) – with heads of creamy white flowers, you might look for pink lilies to set in pots in front of it. In the end, it is all about weight. You do not want too much of it, which is why it is a grave mistake to jam a load of purple plants together, unleavened by other colours. And you need to be more careful with purple foliage than you do with flowers. The flowers are evanescent, but the foliage will be with you for months. Never be afraid to experiment, though, and never be afraid to gamble. Unexpected success is far sweeter than certainty.

The bright blooms of self-seeding poppies light up a summer border where the vigorous *Geranium pratense* 'Mrs Kendall Clark' flowers between feathery plumes of bronze fennel (*Foeniculum vulgare* 'Giant Bronze').

Used with more ephemeral, showy companions, this handsome astrantia will give pleasure for at least six months of the year. By early autumn it will be looking distinctly shabby, and it is best to shear down the foliage then, ready for a fresh start in spring. The hand-shaped leaves are deeply cut and make sturdy, vigorous clumps. By early summer you will already be seeing the charming, papery flower heads, which stand in good condition for many weeks. The astrantia is the anchor in this group, its elegant, pale colours enlivened first by the burst of airy pink and white flowers from the oenothera (formerly gaura), and then by the late summer flowers of the galtonia, purer and whiter than the astrantia, with its greenish underlay, can ever be. The bulbs have no *raison d'être* except their flowers. The astrantia gives necessary bulk and longevity to the group.

Astrantia major subsp. *involucrata* 'Shaggy' + *Oenothera lindheimeri* / *Galtonia candicans*

---

(1) *Astrantia major* subsp. *involucrata* 'Shaggy' (Masterwort)

HEIGHT: 30–90 cm (12–36 in)

SPREAD: 45 cm (18 in)

FLOWERING TIME: Early to mid-summer

STAR QUALITIES: Papery, greenish-white bracts, very long in this variety, surround tiny greenish-white flowers. Each flower head looks like a miniature posy.

ALTERNATIVES: 'Roma' is a vigorous mid-pink variety, selected by the contemporary Dutch designer Piet Oudolf. 'Sunningdale Variegated' has pale pink bracts surrounding greenish flowers held above handsome leaves that are strongly variegated in creamy yellow.

(2) *Oenothera lindheimeri*

A short-lived perennial, generally grown as an annual. It flowers in the first year from seed, producing, over a long season, a succession of small, graceful, pink and white flowers on wiry 90 cm (36 in) stems. On their own, they have a tendency to flop, but the foliage and stems of the astrantia and galtonia will help with support. 'Summer Breeze' and 'The Bride' are both popular selections.

(3) *Galtonia candicans*

Galtonia is a native of the eastern Cape of South Africa, where it gets rain in summer and lies dormant in winter. It is not always easy to establish, but once you see its deliciously waxy white bells, like those of an overgrown summer hyacinth, you want to make every effort to please it. Plant bulbs in early spring, setting them at least 15 cm (6 in) deep, and cut down the flowered stems in autumn. They are slow to increase, but soil well-enriched with rotted compost will help them on their way.

1

2

3

The standard types of border campanulas – *C. lactiflora, C. latiloba* and their like – are not fussy about soil, though most are found on alkaline soil in the wild. They are also very tolerant of shade, though left to themselves they would choose a spot that was in sun for at least part of the day. They enjoy being split and replanted in fresh ground every couple of years. They do not need lush feeding – they are used to fighting for survival – and are wonderfully resilient against pests and disease. The blues of the border campanulas are misty and diluted, excellent with the dramatic cone-shaped flowers of the echinacea. The lime-green heads of the alchemilla will froth round underneath the two taller components of this group, a classic trio for a summer cottage garden.

Campanula lactiflora 'Prichard's Variety' + *Echinacea purpurea* 'White Swan' / *Alchemilla mollis*

① *Campanula lactiflora* 'Prichard's Variety'

HEIGHT: 75 cm (30 in)

SPREAD: 60 cm (24 in)

FLOWERING TIME: Mid- to late summer

STAR QUALITIES: Flowers of an open bell shape, dark violet-blue on strongly branched stems.

ALTERNATIVES: *C. latiloba* 'Percy Piper' has rich lavender blue flowers; 'Hidcote Amethyst' has tall spires of pale amethyst flowers; 'Alba' has pure white flowers.

② *Echinacea purpurea* 'White Swan' (Coneflower)

Stout stems up to 60 cm (24 in) bear white flowers up to 11 cm (4 in) across, each with a prominent, cone-shaped centre of orange-brown. The petals hang down around the cone, giving echinaceas an immediately recognizable silhouette. They like the same growing conditions as the campanulas: good soil in full sun. The foliage is coarse and bristly, but the flowers are excellent for cutting. Butterflies love them.

③ *Alchemilla mollis* (Lady's mantle)

Alchemilla ranks as one of the most useful of all groundcover plants – common but indispensable. Its only vice is an over-enthusiastic urge to procreate. Be ruthless with self-sown seedlings, or avoid them altogether by cutting down the flower heads before they seed. The leaves are shallowly lobed and fairly hairy. Their most endearing characteristic is the way they hold drops of water, rolling them round like small balls of mercury.

2

3

If you are lucky (that is to say, if the weather is kind), the California poppies (*Eschscholzia*) will continue to provide a background of brilliant oranges and yellows for both the allium in high summer and the ceratostigma, which starts to flower a little later. All these plants like sun, as much as they can get. The flowers of the ceratostigma are a wonderful clear cobalt blue, a favourite with hummingbird hawkmoths and other insects seeking late summer nectar. It is a spreading shrub, usually wider (1.5 m / 5 ft) than it is high, with neatly pointed leaves on twiggy growth. In autumn the foliage turns red, an extra bonus. Although top growth may get cut down in a harsh winter, it is generous with new shoots from the base. The allium has tall stems but relatively small flower heads of a good, clear blue. It will sit easily among the finely dissected grey foliage of the Californian poppies, whose exuberant flowering is brought to an end only by frost.

Ceratostigma willmottianum + *Allium caeruleum* / *Eschscholzia californica*

---

(1) *Ceratostigma willmottianum*

HEIGHT: 1 m (3 ft)

SPREAD: 1.5 m (5 ft)

FLOWERING TIME: Late summer to autumn

STAR QUALITIES: A scatter of flowers of an arresting bright blue. Small, pointed leaves that turn bright red in autumn. A neat, twiggy habit.

ALTERNATIVES: *C. plumbaginoides* is a woody-based perennial, not a shrub. It has similar blue flowers, but they are smaller and borne in spikes rather than scattered singly.

(2) *Allium caeruleum*

An unusual colour for an allium, with golf ball-sized flowers that may be made up of at least forty individual florets. The dried heads stand well on their stems when flowering has finished. Plant the bulbs in clusters quite close together, so the lovely blue shimmers in clouds above the California poppies.

(3) *Eschscholzia californica* (California poppy)

For instant effect you can scarcely beat the annual California poppy. To start them off, you simply scatter the seed and wait. Pyramid-shaped buds burst open to reveal silky poppy flowers in a dazzling array of sunset colours. After the first season, they will self-sow, though the mixed oranges and yellows you started with will gradually drift back to the plain brilliant orange of the wild species. The foliage is also excellent: finely cut and bluish-grey.

2

3

Cerinthe was originally a native of the Mediterranean area but took the gardening world by storm when it was reintroduced in an improved, subtle, purple-flowered form from New Zealand. It is an annual, and though it self-seeds, the seedlings are not always tough enough to make it through winter. Cerinthe is used to a Mediterranean climate, and will certainly be able to look after itself in areas which do not have too many severe frosts in winter; otherwise, you will have to raise fresh plants from seed each year. The hosta, when it arrives, will give bulk to the group and a long succession of mauve flowers that will tone with the cerinthe's bizarre flower heads. This group has nothing for winter, but that may not matter, especially if there is a clump of *Euphorbia amygdaloides* var. *robbiae* (see p.34) or some other evergreen nearby to take your eye away from the gap. Triteleia gives an enchanting lift in mid-summer.

Cerinthe major 'Purpurascens' + *Hosta* 'Lemon Lime' / *Triteleia laxa* 'Koningin Fabiola'

---

① *Cerinthe major* 'Purpurascens'

HEIGHT: 60 cm (24 in)

SPREAD: 30 cm (12 in)

FLOWERING TIME: Early to late summer

STAR QUALITIES: Fleshy, slightly glaucous foliage. Strange, drooping flower heads that sometimes seem steely grey, sometimes ultramarine, mauve or purple, saturated and exotic.

ALTERNATIVES: The standard species has pale grey-green leaves blotched with white and bluish bracts enclosing tubular yellow flowers.

② *Hosta* 'Lemon Lime'

The only problem with hostas is that slugs dote on them as much as gardeners do. Prepare to defend the lush spikes when they first push through the ground. There are hundreds of varieties to choose from; this one has dainty foliage, no more than 10 cm (4 in) long. It grows vigorously, with leaves that are yellow at the tips, shading to lime-green towards the stalks. A succession of purplish flowers striped with white are produced during summer on stems 30 cm (12 in) long.

③ *Triteleia laxa* 'Koningin Fabiola'

Think of an agapanthus shrunk in the wash, and you will have some idea of what this plant looks like. Loose clusters of tubular blue flowers spring from stalks that can be up to 60 cm (24 in) high. They flower in mid-summer, just before agapanthus, and being natives of California, they like warm, sunny spots in the garden. Plant the corms about 8 cm (3 in) deep in autumn.

3

1

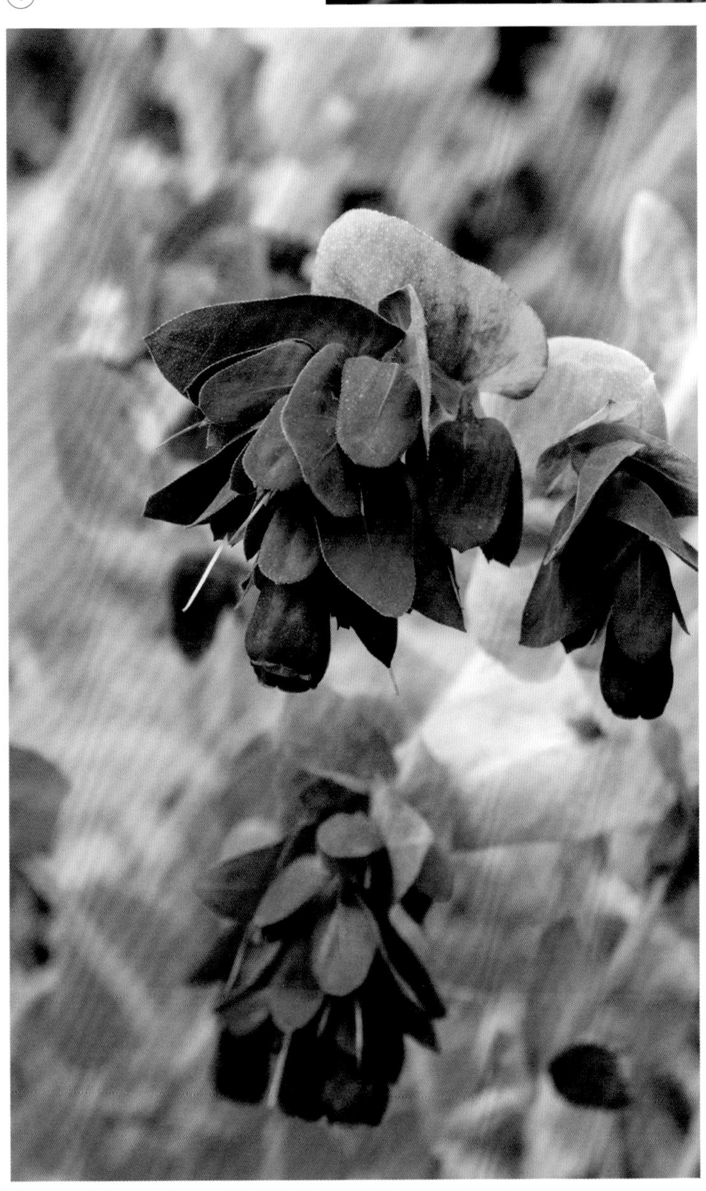

2

Crocosmia leaves are almost as good as those of an iris, though they do not have quite the same stiff, upright formality and are a greener green, without that glaucous overlay that makes the iris stand out so well. But the crocosmia has something the iris does not have: ribbing, made by pleats running lengthways down the leaf. These long ribs are the leaf's scaffolding. Even in spring, crocosmia leaves are advanced and handsome enough to make useful landmarks between camassias and mounds of brunnera. When the crocosmia produces its brilliant crimson sprays, it will be partnered by the grass (*Calamagrostis brachytrica*). The indefatigable nasturtiums, which will have started to flower in June, will charge on into autumn with wonderfully reckless abandon. Hungry gardeners should note that leaves of nasturtium are good to eat, as are nasturtium seeds when green and peppery.

Crocosmia 'Hellfire' + *Calamagrostis brachytrica* / *Tropaeolum majus* 'Empress of India'

1. *Crocosmia* 'Hellfire'

HEIGHT: 1–1.2 m (3–4 ft)

SPREAD: 75 cm (30 in)

FLOWERING TIME: Mid- to late summer

STAR QUALITIES: Robust habit of growth. Brilliant red flowers, a deeper colour than 'Lucifer', both of them bigger and more effective than old kinds of what used to be called 'montbretia'. This variety also has handsome pleated leaves.

ALTERNATIVES: *C.* × *crocosmiiflora* 'Babylon' has brilliant red flowers marked with maroon in the centre; *C.* × *crocosmiiflora* 'Star of the East' has golden orange flowers, each with a yellow eye; *C. masoniorum* has mid-green leaves and orange-red flowers.

2. *Calamagrostis brachytrica* (Foxtail grass)

A strongly upright grass, making dense clumps of narrow leaves that arch out from the centre. In late summer, flowering stems, up to 90–150 cm (3–5 ft) push up from the foliage, bearing silvery-grey heads, narrow in outline, that fluff up and stand for a long while into winter. The clumps can be cut back in early spring before new growth starts to show.

3. *Tropaeolum majus* 'Empress of India'

This is a bushy nasturtium (so called after watercress, *Nasturtium officinale*, because of the similarity of their taste), not a climbing one, and it has wonderful foliage of deep blue-green. Nothing could be a better background for the flowers, which are a deep blood-red, sumptuous and velvety. It is the most lustrous and beautiful of all nasturtiums.

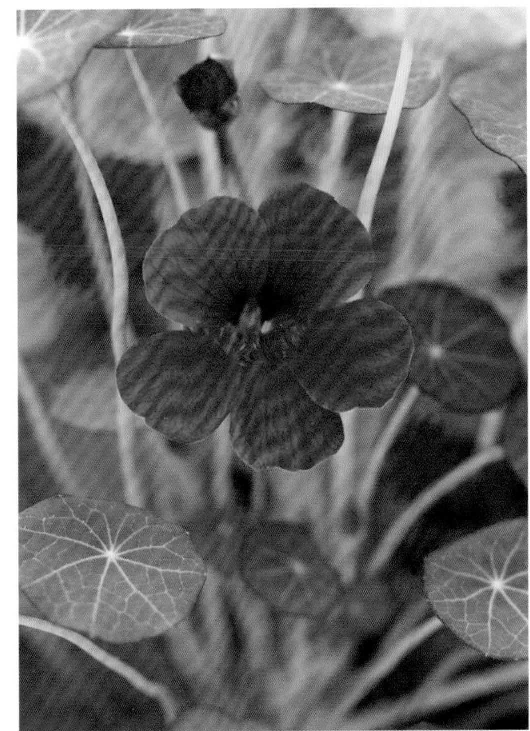

3

2

1

The vast Pacific Hybrid delphiniums, with spikes up to 2 m (6 ft), are showy but not the easiest plants to use in a garden: they are top-heavy and require firm staking. Easier in mixed groups is the looser, airier *D. grandiflorum*, which is a short-lived perennial, generally used as an annual. The blue of delphiniums can scarcely be matched by any other flower. It is a clear, clean blue, beautifully set off against its own pale green foliage. If you use delphiniums with white cosmos and spikes of purple lupins, the effect will be cool and restrained. Changing the scheme to include pink cosmos instead of white will warm up the whole combination. This is very much a summer group and both the cosmos and the delphinium will provide plenty of flowers for picking. These three will all be out together, but when they have finished, there will be nothing for autumn or spring. You could fill the spring gap by adding sweetly scented jonquils or bluebells around the newly emerging foliage of the lupins.

Delphinium grandiflorum 'Blue Butterfly' + *Cosmos bipinnatus* 'Sonata White' / *Lupinus* 'Thundercloud'

---

(1) *Delphinium grandiflorum* 'Blue Butterfly'

HEIGHT: 50 cm (20 in)

SPREAD: 30 cm (12 in)

FLOWERING TIME: Early to mid-summer

STAR QUALITIES: Light, airy growth with flowers of a clear, bright blue. Ferny foliage. They are more natural in style than the monster spikes of exhibition delphiniums.

ALTERNATIVES: This type of delphinium may be listed as *Consolida regalis* (larkspur) 'Blue Cloud'. The Belladonna Group of delphiniums are similarly light and open in growth, but much taller.

(2) *Cosmos bipinnatus* 'Sonata White'

This is an annual that looks as though it should be a perennial, with finely cut foliage and showy, saucer-shaped flowers. The Sonata Series produces flowers that are shorter than most cosmos. It is suggested here because it will match the shortish delphinium in height. If you use a taller delphinium, perhaps one of the Belladonna Group, you could use a bigger cosmos, such as 'Purity' or the semi-double 'Fizzy White', both of which grow to 1 m (3 ft).

(3) *Lupinus* 'Thundercloud'

Lupins have foliage that is as good as their flowers, the leaves deeply cut into a round whorl of leaflets, joined together at the stem. Their heyday was the 1930s, when the lupins newly raised by George Russell of York were a stately component of many herbaceous borders. After the main spike has finished flowering in mid-summer, side spikes continue the display for several more weeks.

1

2

3

This particular deutzia is one of the most enchanting shrubs of high summer. It grows slowly to about 2 m (6 ft), the rough, dull green foliage sprinkled thickly all over with specks of white as the buds begin to form. Dazzlingly white flowers open in succession in the second half of summer, individually small but produced in breathtaking profusion. Overall, the structure of the shrub is rather delicate, upright rather than spreading, and it looks best with companions that are not too beefy. The hosta 'Halcyon', with its cool, grey, pointed leaves, would fit in well as an underplanting, as it is not too tall. 'Halcyon's lavender-coloured flowers come towards the end of summer, when the deutzia's have finished, so together the pair would provide quite a long season of interest. For spring, add a sprinkle of bulbs such as the pale powder-blue grape hyacinth *Muscari armeniacum* 'Valerie Finnis' or its madder relative *M. comosum* 'Plumosum' – a dark purplish-blue creation that looks as if it is unravelling before your eyes.

Deutzia setchuenensis var. *corymbiflora* 'Kiftsgate' + *Hosta* 'Halcyon' / *Muscari comosum* 'Plumosum'

(1) *Deutzia setchuenensis* var. *corymbiflora* 'Kiftsgate'

HEIGHT: 2 m (6 ft)

SPREAD: 1.5 m (5 ft)

FLOWERING TIME: High summer

STAR QUALITIES: A delicate shrub, smothered with small, star-shaped flowers of startlingly pure white.

ALTERNATIVES: *D. gracilis* 'Nikko' is much smaller, with white flowers and leaves that turn purplish-red in autumn; *D.* × *hybrida* 'Mont Rose' flowers earlier with purplish-pink flowers.

(2) *Hosta* 'Halcyon'

The leaves are bright blue-grey and at 20 cm (8 in) long, not overwhelming. 'Halcyon' is one of the neat Tardiana Group of hostas and bears dense stems of flower in late summer, about 45 cm (18 in) tall. They are lavender-grey, so the whole effect is very muted. The leaves collapse with the first frost but return early the following spring.

(3) *Muscari comosum* 'Plumosum' (Grape hyacinth)

This is a completely bizarre grape hyacinth that, at the moment of flowering, forgets what it set out to do. Instead of producing the tight little bells we are used to in a grape hyacinth, it erupts into a fluff of tiny purplish threads, disarming and appealing. The leaves are no more than 15 cm (6 in) long, but the flowers top them by a good 5 cm (2 in).

2

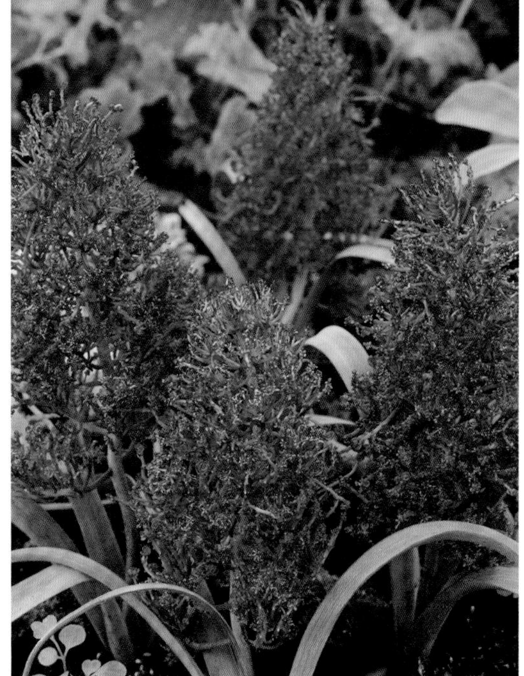

3

Only the dianthus in this group will make a mark for twelve months of the year. The mats of foliage may become slightly weather-beaten through winter, but in spring, new shoots will freshen the plants and accompany the emerging foliage of the aquilegias. The early effect will be pale grey-green, embellished in mid-summer when the dianthus first produces its pink-fringed blooms. If you deadhead the dianthus, it will produce more flowers, sporadically, later in the season. The aquilegia needs to be cut down quite severely when it has finished flowering. It will make fresh mounds of foliage that will be useful fillers between the less substantial stems of the hare's tail grass. Although this is only an annual, it has a long season, and even in autumn the fluffy terminal spikes will be intriguing enough to demand attention.

Dianthus 'Gran's Favourite' + *Aquilegia* 'Hensol Harebell' / *Lagurus ovatus*

① *Dianthus* 'Gran's Favourite'

HEIGHT: 35 cm (14 in)

SPREAD: 35 cm (14 in)

FLOWERING TIME: Mid-summer onwards

STAR QUALITIES: Neat mats of grey foliage, topped by double flowers of white, fringed and centred with deep purplish-red. They are deliciously scented.

ALTERNATIVES: *D.* 'Dad's Favourite', an old-fashioned laced pink with semi-double white flowers, edged and centred with purple; *D. alpinus* 'Joan's Blood', with dark green foliage and single, deep magenta flowers; *D.* 'Hidcote', with mats of grey foliage setting off splendidly rich red double flowers.

② *Aquilegia* 'Hensol Harebell'

One of the few rules in gardening is that you can never have too many aquilegias. The foliage – greyish and slightly glaucous – is beautiful in itself and furnishes the ground from early spring. Aquilegias with long spurs floating back from the frilly cups are slightly more difficult to keep than short-spurred types. In this short-spurred cultivar, the flowers are a gorgeous soft blue on stems up to 75 cm (30 in). It was raised in the early 1900s by Mrs Kennedy at Mossdale, Castle Douglas, in Scotland.

③ *Lagurus ovatus* (Hare's tail grass)

In the wild, this pretty grass grows in sandy soil in Spain and other Mediterranean countries, flowering between mid-spring and early summer. In cooler climates and grown from spring-sown seed, its flowering will be later. The stems may grow to 50 cm (20 in) but are generally shorter, each tipped with the rounded, softly hairy heads that give the grass its common name. It dries well. For the best results, pick it before the heads are fully mature.

3

2

1

You need a hot, sunny, dry position for these plants, all of which have the bleached-out look of creatures used to desert conditions. It is a group to be planted mostly for form and contrasts of foliage. The fine sea holly will be the dominant feature, but it is a biennial. Be prepared to stop up gaps by having some young plants in reserve. It is also a vigorous self-seeder: equilibrium will eventually be achieved, and plantings will renew themselves without your guidance. The skeletal plants dry well, but they will also stand in the garden for a long time during autumn and early winter, before birds finally pick the domed seed heads to pieces. Both the pelargonium and the echeveria are greenhouse plants, and they can only be set out in the garden when all danger of frost has passed. In temperate climates, this usually means late spring. They will then get better and better until you start to worry about frost again in early autumn and whisk them back under cover. So this is an ephemeral planting, but it offers plenty of scope for change and renewal. You might experiment with aeoniums instead of echeverias, or use a different pelargonium, such as 'Pink Capricorn'. It has bigger, showier flowers than most other scented-leaved pelargoniums, in a deep, rich pink.

Eryngium giganteum + *Pelargonium* 'Lady Plymouth' / *Echeveria elegans*

1. *Eryngium giganteum* (Miss Willmott's ghost / Sea holly)

HEIGHT: 90 cm (36 in)

SPREAD: 30 cm (12 in)

FLOWERING TIME: Mid- to late summer

STAR QUALITIES: Spiny, stiff habit, which gives architectural structure to a plant group. Steely blue-grey bracts surround flowers domed like teasels. Long-lasting.

ALTERNATIVES: *E. bourgatii* 'Picos Blue', with flower heads of a stunning, rich blue; *E.* × *oliverianum*, which has thin, linear bracts of purplish-silver; *E.* × *tripartitum*, which has relatively inconspicuous bracts and neat rounded heads of flower in a plant of open, branching habit.

2. *Pelargonium* 'Lady Plymouth'

Scented-leaved pelargoniums such as this are grown more for their foliage than their flowers. *P.* 'Lady Plymouth' has finely cut leaves with creamy margins, which when touched, release pungent waves of eucalyptus. It grows 30–40 cm (12–16 in) tall, the inconspicuous lavender-pink flowers borne from mid- to late summer. It is not hardy and in areas of frost needs to be brought under cover for winter.

3. *Echeveria elegans*

Succulent, fat echeverias look as though they have been made of wax, each leaf perfectly placed to make a symmetrical rosette that spreads gently with age. They are slow starters, but by the end of the summer plump themselves up at an astonishing rate. They are not hardy, but bring an exotic air to a plant group.

3

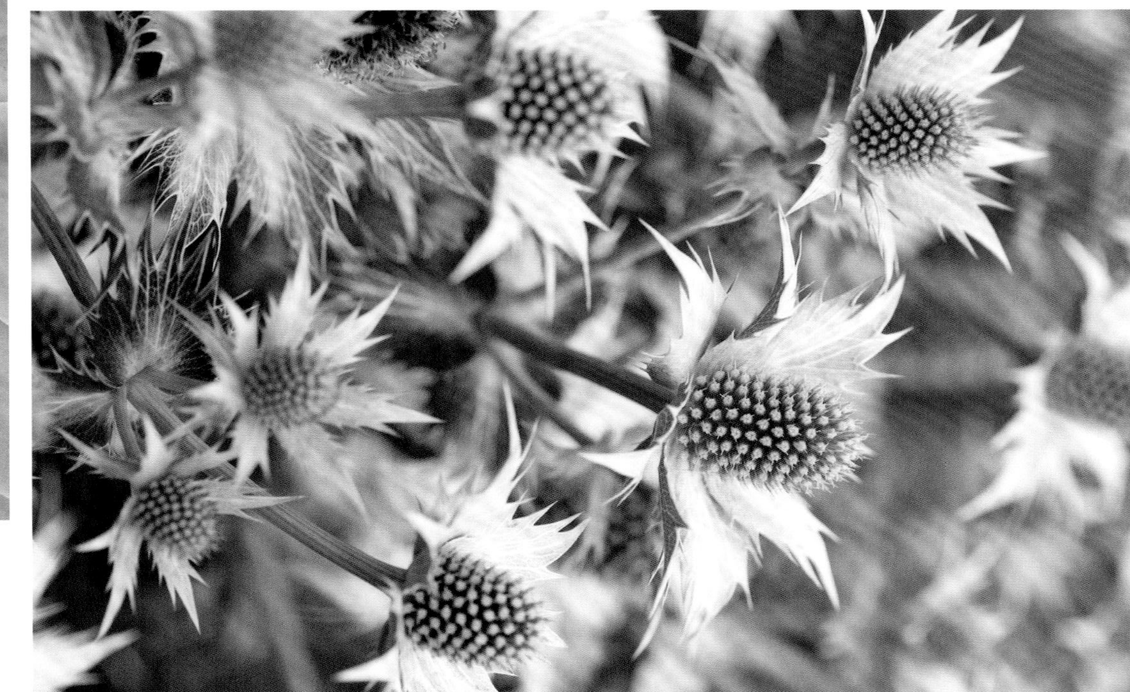

Fuchsias are wonderfully long-flowering shrubs, excellent players in a late summer garden. Some varieties are wildly theatrical, pirouetting with many-skirted flowers in bright pinks and purples. *F. magellanica* is a species native to Chile and Argentina and has the loose grace typical of plants left as nature intended. Lax branches arch out from the base, bearing thin flowers of deep red that swing and sway on the stems. They will last until the first frosts. The tall-growing salvia with its rich, deep blue flowers provides a fine contrast. Some plants can push up between the thin branches of the fuchsia, others reach up behind. The flowering spikes stand strongly upright, tapering gracefully to the tip. It is not absolutely hardy, but you can take cuttings as a precaution. The magenta gladiolus will flower in early summer and set the tone for the fuchsia, which follows later in the season. All these plants will do best in a sunny, open situation.

Fuchsia magellanica + *Salvia* 'Indigo Spires' / *Gladiolus communis* subsp. *byzantinus*

(1) *Fuchsia magellanica*

HEIGHT: 2–3 m (6 10 ft)

SPREAD: 2–3 m (6–10 ft)

FLOWERING TIME: High summer to autumn

STAR QUALITIES: Not as immediately showy as some garden varieties, but easier to use in a mixed planting. Exceptionally long period in flower. Elegant, relaxed growth habit. Blooms of rich, deep red.

ALTERNATIVES: *F.* 'Alice Hoffman' has bronze foliage and semi-double flowers in pink and white; 'Dollar Prinzessin' is upright in growth, with double flowers in cerise and purple; 'Mrs Lovell Swisher', with red and white flowers, is more tender, but vigorous and free-flowering.

(2) *Salvia* 'Indigo Spires'

This handsome hybrid between *S. farinacea* and *S. longispicata* arose in the Huntington Botanical Gardens in California. In cooler climates it is not reliably hardy, but it can be kept going if you take cuttings in late summer. It grows to about 1.5 m (5 ft), the dark purplish-blue flowers borne on stems suffused with the same dark colouring. Growth is vigorous, and the plants make imposingly leafy clumps.

(3) *Gladiolus communis* subsp. *byzantinus*

This wild gladiolus, a native of Spain and northwest Africa, is a world away from the top-heavy gladioli of the show bench. It grows like a herbaceous plant, self-supporting and strongly upright in growth. It is lovely in bud, when the whole flower head turns over in an elegant curve. Most gladioli produce their flowers on one side of the spike only; this one has flowers that face sideways as well as forward. There may be up to twenty of them on a spike, appearing from early summer onwards.

3

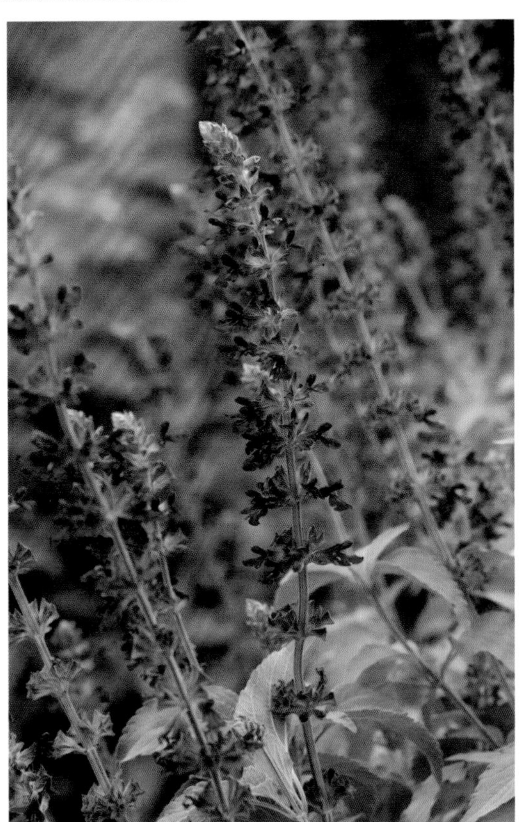

2

The term 'groundcover' is often used rather despairingly, as though it were a last resort, like linoleum in the bathroom. But when well-used, groundcover plants are among the most interesting of garden plants, because they lend themselves to so many different planting schemes. They need not be baldly utilitarian, but can be knitted into groups of different colours and textures that ebb and flow through the seasons to give different effects at different times of the year. Geraniums are brilliant groundcover plants, and *G. psilostemon* adds to its handsome foliage arresting flowers of brilliant magenta produced over several months in summer. Use it with dramatic *Angelica gigas*, which bears flat, purple flower heads in late summer on equally lustrous stems. Fill in with a lush planting of 'Spring Green' tulips to hold the ground while the geranium is beginning to leaf up in spring. Tulips provide as pleasant a way to bankrupt yourself as any other, and are so much better for your liver than alcohol.

Geranium psilostemon + *Angelica gigas* / *Tulipa* 'Spring Green'

---

1 *Geranium psilostemon*

HEIGHT: 60–120 cm (2–4 ft)

SPREAD: 60 cm (24 in)

FLOWERING TIME: Early to late summer

STAR QUALITIES: Generous, ground-covering foliage, a good foil for other plants. Tall, eye-catching stems of brilliant magenta flowers, each with a black eye. Long lasting.

ALTERNATIVES: *G.* 'Ann Folkard', a scrambler rather than a clumper, but with flowers of a similar style and colour; *G. cinereum* 'Ballerina', an alpine geranium, producing dwarf rosettes topped with purplish-red flowers, useful where space is too limited for the magisterial *G. psilostemon*.

2 *Angelica gigas*

Biennial, like the common angelica, but *A. gigas* is blessed with stems and flowering heads of moody purple, rather than pale green. The flowering only happens in the second year. For the first year, the plant concentrates on building huge mounds of foliage through which the geranium can scramble. Where suited – in damp, heavy soil – the flowering stems can reach 2 m (6 ft); the flowers come later than those of the ordinary green angelica.

3 *Tulipa* 'Spring Green'

'Spring Green' is a Viridiflora tulip, with a broad green flame up the centre of each petal, showing both on the back and the front. Extremely cool and elegant, the green flames are set against a ground of creamy white. The anthers are pale green too. Each petal has a slight sideways twist on it.

3

Bright yellow daisies are an essential feature of a late summer garden. They are also favourite components in the new style of 'prairie planting', in which huge swathes of perennials are planted in interlocking groups and grown with minimal intervention on the part of the gardener. The style originated in the public parks of Germany, and for the full effect, you need plenty of space. Prairie plants of North America, such as the helenium and the rudbeckia, are, of course, ideal for this kind of treatment and blaze out together in the second half of summer with complementary daisy flowers of mahogany and yellow. The inner disc of the rudbeckia flower matches the rich brownish-red of *Helenium* 'Moerheim Beauty'. The spurge flowers much earlier, in late spring and early summer, but its brick-coloured flower heads will add their own strong contribution to the later sunburned colours of the daisies.

Helenium 'Moerheim Beauty' + *Rudbeckia fulgida* var. *sullivantii* 'Goldsturm' / *Euphorbia griffithii* 'Dixter'

(1) *Helenium* 'Moerheim Beauty'

HEIGHT: 90 cm (36 in)

SPREAD: 60 cm (24 in)

FLOWERING TIME: Mid- to late summer

STAR QUALITIES: Rich copper-red flowers, the petals swept back from the central dark cone. Sturdy growth habit.

ALTERNATIVES: *H.* 'Baudirektor Linne' is taller, with velvety, brownish-red flowers; 'Bruno' has a markedly upright habit, with petals of the same brownish-red round a darker centre; 'Rubinzwerg' has dark red petals around a rich brown centre.

(2) *Rudbeckia fulgida* var. *sullivantii* 'Goldsturm' (Coneflower)

The rudbeckias are an easy-going group of plants that provide a generous display of yellow daisy flowers. They are ideal elements in a relaxed, prairie-style planting that might include grasses or red-hot pokers as well as the plants suggested here. 'Goldsturm' has narrow orange-yellow petals falling away from a dark central disc. It was a favourite of the famous German nurseryman Karl Foerster who, in the 1930s, was one of the founding fathers of the New Perennial movement.

(3) *Euphorbia griffithii* 'Dixter'

The great English gardener Christopher Lloyd, who died in 2006, picked out this seedling from a batch growing at Washfield Nursery, near his home at Great Dixter in Sussex. The foliage is much redder in this type than in the more common species and provides a suitably hot setting for the flowers, which are brick-coloured. The form 'Fireglow' has the same orange-red flowers, but set against green foliage.

1

3

2

Cool, damp soil suits all three of these plants, none of which will be crying out for sun. To get the best effect from the foliage of the hosta, the ground needs to be rich in humus too. If you can provide these conditions, this group may well draw you back more often than any other plants in the garden. It is a cool combination, because even the yellow of the primula is a sharp, frosty yellow, muted by the downy meal that covers its flower heads. The hosta is one of the best of this huge family because the leaves, neither too big nor too wide, are carried well above the ground, swelling out from strong stems to make pewter-coloured vases. The solidity of the hosta foliage is offset by the more intricately cut leaves of the monkshood (*Aconitum*). It's a poisonous plant, but who would want to eat it anyway? Just take care handling it. For a cooler effect use the grey-flowered monkshood 'Stainless Steel' rather than the blue.

Hosta 'Krossa Regal' + *Aconitum* 'Bressingham Spire' / *Primula florindae*

① *Hosta* 'Krossa Regal'

HEIGHT: 70 cm (28 in)

SPREAD: 75 cm (30 in)

FLOWERING TIME: Summer

STAR QUALITIES: Large, glaucous, bluish-green leaves, held well above the ground on long stalks. Elegant sheaves of pale lilac flowers. Has the potential eventually to make clumps 1.5 m (5 ft) across.

ALTERNATIVES: *H.* 'Blue Angel' has bigger leaves and white flowers; 'Frances Williams' is a subtle bicolour, with blue-green leaves edged in a yellowish green. To accentuate the yellow in this group, use a golden-leaved cultivar such as *H.* 'Wind River Gold' or 'Zounds'.

② *Aconitum* 'Bressingham Spire' (Monkshood)

The monkshoods are an incredibly handsome group of plants, with dark, slightly lustrous foliage, intricately cut, and tall spikes of hooded flowers. Many of the selections are in shades of blue, like 'Bressingham Spire', which has dark, slightly violet blooms. It grows sturdily upright to about 1 m (3 ft), flowering towards the end of summer. Use the hosta to disguise foliage at the base of the monkshoods, which by this time is beginning to die off.

③ *Primula florindae* (Giant cowslip)

One of the latest of the primulas to bloom, bearing in summer drooping heads of acid-yellow flowers, sometimes as many as forty on a single stem. The petals are powdered with white meal. It is powerful enough to suppress annual weeds with its big, meaty clumps of leaves. Its home is Tibet, where it grows in marshy ground and along the banks of streams. Give it damp ground. It is deliciously scented.

2

3

These hydrangeas need space, as they can eventually grow up to 3 m (10 ft) high. They earn every inch. *H. aspera* subsp. *sargentiana* was brought into cultivation in 1908 by the plant hunter Ernest 'Chinese' Wilson from an expedition funded by the Arnold Arboretum, part of Harvard University. As a thank you, Wilson named this magnificent hydrangea after his near contemporary, the arboretum's director Charles Sprague Sargent. It has huge, paddle-shaped leaves the texture of sharkskin, and flower heads that are at least 30 cm (12 in) across, flat and filled in the middle with tiny pinkish-mauve flowers. Each flower has stamens of a searingly bright blue. Arranged round the edge of each head in a haphazard way are the sterile florets, white tinged with mauve. The whole thing looks quite rigid, as the huge flower heads are held on stiff, hairy stems. It grows best in quite deep shade. The foxgloves will provide excitement before the hydrangea gets going, and the beautiful shuttlecock fern can erupt quietly under the hydrangea's branches.

Hydrangea aspera subsp. *sargentiana* + *Digitalis purpurea* 'Sutton's Apricot' / *Matteuccia struthiopteris*

(1) *Hydrangea aspera* subsp. *sargentiana*

HEIGHT: 3 m (10 ft)

SPREAD: 2.2 m (7 ft)

FLOWERING TIME: Late summer to autumn

STAR QUALITIES: Imposing foliage, stiffly dramatic. Enormous flattish flower heads drifting through white and pink and blue. Sparse, sculptural presence in winter.

ALTERNATIVES: *H. aspera* Villosa Group has narrower leaves of a velvety dark green and similar, flattish flower heads; *H. arborescens* 'Annabelle' has enormous white balls of flower.

(2) *Digitalis purpurea* 'Sutton's Apricot'

This foxglove is a biennial, producing a fat rosette of leaves the first year and shooting up for a full performance in the second. It produces tall, elegant spikes of flower, excellent in dappled shade. Like other biennials, such as evening primrose, foxgloves will self-seed once they are established. 'Sutton's Apricot' is one of the most ravishing, but you can introduce other types, such as spotted 'Camelot Cream', or mixtures such as the 'Excelsior' hybrids.

(3) *Matteuccia struthiopteris* (Shuttlecock fern)

These ferns erupt gently in spring to make elegant vase-shaped specimens, upright and bright, light green until autumn frosts change them to tones of yellow. They are supremely graceful and not difficult if you can provide a home that is moist but not waterlogged, in the dappled shade under shrubs or trees. They are at their most beautiful when just emerging, each frond curled like a bishop's crozier.

1

2

3

Since lilies hate to be disturbed, it is worth spending time in getting their home right before you plant them. Plenty of humus combined with excellent drainage gives the best results. *Lilium regale* is one of the best-known of all lilies, because compared with other white lilies such as the Madonna lily or Japanese lilies of the *L. auratum* type, it is accommodating. Plant the scaly bulbs in autumn or spring and mulch them annually in spring with leaf mould or well-rotted compost.

Underground slugs are the lilies' worst enemy. Set the bulbs on sharp gritty sand when you plant them, and surround them with more grit as you cover them up. Arrange to have this group by a seat in the garden, so that in the evening you can swim in the scent; the cocktail of lily and tobacco flower will be far more intoxicating than wine. There are a few tobacco flowers with no scent that are worth using, such as *N.* 'Lime Green'. Otherwise, avoid them.

Lilium regale + *Nicotiana sylvestris* / *Visnaga daucoides*

① *Lilium regale*

HEIGHT: 1 m (3 ft)

SPREAD: 30 cm (12 in)

FLOWERING TIME: Mid-summer

STAR QUALITIES: Beautifully scented white trumpets, washed over on the backs of the petals with purplish-pink. Easy to grow in most soils except very alkaline ones.

ALTERNATIVES: Swing the group into pink mode by using a lily such as 'Barbara North' with scented, Turk's cap flowers; the white Madonna lily, *L. candidum*, is beautiful but not so easy to grow as *L. regale.*

② *Nicotiana sylvestris*

This group of plants is named after Jean Nicot, an ambassador who introduced tobacco into France in the sixteenth century. There are many different kinds. *N. sylvestris* is a tall, wild species from Agentina, reaching 1.5 m (5 ft), with long-tubed white flowers, beautifully scented, hanging from the heads. The best scent in this family comes from white flowers, but it is much stronger in the evening than during the day.

③ *Visnaga daucoides*

Umbellifers are wonderful fillers in a garden. *V. daucoides* is an airy, elegant annual with feathery foliage and beautiful domed flower heads of white tinged with green. Grow plenty, because they make excellent cut flowers. The biggest plants come from a late summer sowing, but these will flower in early summer. For plants to peak later, a spring sowing is best. If you do not want to bother with seed, buy seedlings instead. Species, such as this visnaga (formerly *Ammi visnaga*) and the accompanying tobacco plants, give a pleasingly natural air to a garden – not exactly wild, but comfortable and relaxed, as well as beautiful.

3

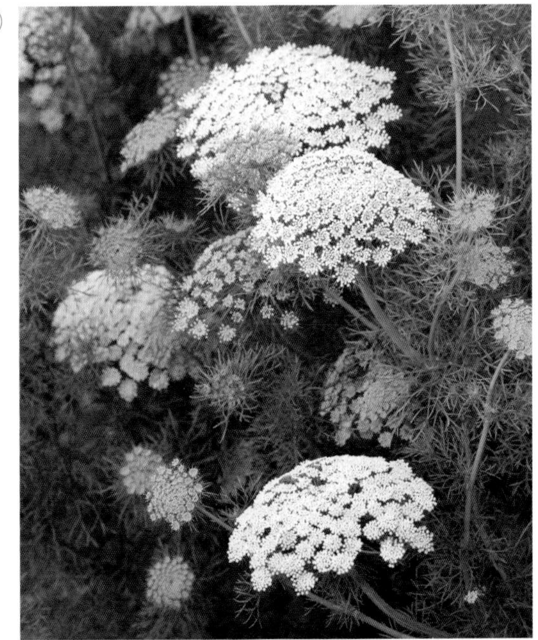

1

2

Love-in-a-mist was introduced from Damascus more than 400 years ago and has remained a popular cottage garden flower ever since. The swollen seed pods are an intriguing feature when the display of flowers comes to an end. They can be cut, dried and used in decorations. In this group, it is best to get the two low-growing perennials, the stachys and the viola, established before you introduce the nigella, which is an annual, growing from fresh seed each year. Prepare the seedbed carefully, in between the other plants, breaking down any intractable lumps of soil. Sow the seed thinly in mid-spring, and cover with a fine scattering of soil. If necessary, thin the seedlings as they emerge, to allow each to develop properly. In suitable soils, the plants will self-seed, saving you the bother of replacing them each year. If self-seeding does not happen, seize the opportunity to try something different – cornflowers perhaps, or a bright scattering of marigolds or California poppies (see p.120).

Nigella damascena 'Miss Jekyll' + *Stachys byzantina* / *Viola* 'Belmont Blue'

① *Nigella damascena* 'Miss Jekyll' (Love-in-a-mist)

HEIGHT: 45 cm (18 in)

SPREAD: 23 cm (9 in)

FLOWERING TIME: Summer

STAR QUALITIES: Sky blue flowers surrounded by a ruff of finely divided tendrils. An excellent flower for cutting. An annual, but generally self-seeds profusely. Fine, filigree foliage and good seed heads, like small balloons. They also dry well.

ALTERNATIVES: *N. hispanica* is a fine dark blue species, the centres of each flower a showy wine colour where the stamens meet in a crown. Taller and wider spreading than *N. damascena*.

② *Stachys byzantina* (Lambs' ears)

Although it can look bedraggled in winter or after heavy summer rain, this is an excellent plant. It prefers well-drained soil, for like many of the greys, it will rot away if it is too damp. It needs picking over regularly, so that the yellowing and withered leaves do not spoil the overall effect. *S.* 'Silver Carpet' is a good non-flowering form of this well-known groundcover plant.

③ *Viola* 'Belmont Blue'

The violas are a vast family, embracing the large monkey-faced pansies as well as tiny wildlings such as *V. odorata*. *V.* 'Belmont Blue' (syn. 'Boughton Blue') is a good, clear blue and, like so many of this tribe, profligate with its flowers. To keep up their superhuman display they need feeding and regular deadheading. If plants get leggy, cut the stems back to a joint close to the base. Shear back the entire plant in late summer.

1

2

3

The colours of the phlox and penstemon have the comfortable familiarity of blue and white china. The salvia introduces a darker, richer tone to the group and ensures that it will continue to have interest until early autumn. There is potential for change, of course. If you substituted pink and white *Penstemon* 'Appleblossom' for the blue *P.* 'Alice Hindley' and used a deep pink salvia such as *S. involucrata* 'Hadspen' instead of 'Caradonna', you would shift the group into a much warmer mode. Phloxes like hefty meals, so in autumn you should mulch the cut-down plants with well-rotted manure or compost. The clumps will need splitting and replanting every few years, in autumn or spring. Get rid of all the woody growth and replant only the vigorous new pieces growing round the sides of the clump. Leave the top growth of the penstemon to provide a little protection to the crown of the plant through winter.

Phlox paniculata 'David' + *Salvia nemorosa* 'Caradonna' / *Penstemon* 'Alice Hindley'

(1) *Phlox paniculata* 'David'

HEIGHT: 90 cm (36 in)

SPREAD: 75 cm (30 in)

FLOWERING TIME: Summer to early autumn

STAR QUALITIES: Dense heads of flower, washing-powder white. Strong constitution. Gives a charming, cottage garden air to any group. Has some resistance to mildew.

ALTERNATIVES: *P. paniculata* 'Fujiyama' is a distinctive variety with cylindrical heads of white flowers on sturdy stems; 'White Admiral' has shapely heads of equally pure white.

(2) *Salvia nemorosa* 'Caradonna'

The explosion in the breeding of salvias gives gardeners many opportunities to introduce banks of blue and purple into a late summer border. Bees love them, scrambling around among the flowers clustered on stems that will reach 50 cm (20 in). The advantage of the salvias that come from *S. nemorosa* is that they are relatively hardy. 'Caradonna' produces flower spikes of purplish-blue with the same colour staining the stems. Cut down the first flush of flowers and another crop will often carry through to early autumn.

(3) *Penstemon* 'Alice Hindley'

An old cultivar first introduced in 1931, but a continuing favourite because of its large flowers of a delicate mauveish-blue. The flowering stems can reach 90 cm (36 in) and peak towards the end of summer. Unfortunately, they are not reliably hardy. Damp is as big an enemy as frost, and you will please this penstemon by finding it a well-drained spot in full sun. Do not cut down the stems in autumn, as they provide protection for new spring shoots that may otherwise be slaughtered by frost.

3

2

1

This is a combination with a pleasingly natural air, ideal for a pond-side planting or for damp soil in a wilder part of the garden. The iris will be the first of the flowers to bloom in this group, carrying a succession of pale, perfect flowers from early summer. By the time the ligularia and rodgersia come into play, from mid-summer onwards, the iris will have finished. That is just as well, because its own quiet voice would be drowned by the *fortissimo* performance of the others, especially the ligularia, which has uncompromisingly bold flowers. But even without flowers, this group will be worth looking at because all the plants have superb foliage. The roughly hand-shaped leaves of the rodgersia are set against the more rounded outlines of the ligularia foliage. The iris leaves provide punctuation marks among the other mounds, solid uprights eye-catchingly variegated. All enjoy the same damp conditions, but the rodgersia is much slower to bulk up than the ligularia. Do not let it get swamped.

Rodgersia aesculifolia + *Iris laevigata* 'Variegata' / *Ligularia* 'The Rocket'

(1) *Rodgersia aesculifolia*

HEIGHT: 1.2 m (4 ft)

SPREAD: 1 m (3 ft)

FLOWERING TIME: Mid-summer onwards

STAR QUALITIES: Superb foliage, toothed leaflets in hand-shaped clusters, like the horse chestnut that gives it its name. Strong tall panicles of flower with the texture of plush. Both pink and white forms are available.

ALTERNATIVES: *R. pinnata* 'Superba' (see p.78) has similar hand-shaped leaves, heavily burnished with purplish bronze when they first emerge in late spring. *R. podophylla* has jagged leaves and creamy flowers that appear from mid- to late summer.

(2) *Iris laevigata* 'Variegata'

Not so tall as the yellow flag iris (*I. pseudacorus*; see p.96), this iris has striking foliage, growing up to 45 cm (18 in) and striped in soft cream and pale green. This is a variegation that murmurs, rather than shouts, and it is wonderful with the lavender-blue flowers that come out in summer. It needs moist soil and will even grow happily with its feet dangling in water.

(3) *Ligularia* 'The Rocket'

Big rounded leaves with jagged, toothed edges. Grows best where the soil is moist and rich. Both the leaf stalks and the stems bearing the flowers are almost black, a dramatic foil to the brilliant yellow flower heads. These are produced over a long season from early to late summer. All the ligularias are hefty things. They are among the best of all plants for bogs and pool sides.

2

3

Romneya is an extremely handsome late-flowering member of the poppy family, with tall, almost woody stems reaching at least 2 m (6 ft). Its home is California, so it needs a sunny spot with its feet in well-drained soil. After a hard winter the stems may die back, but new growth pushes through as the season warms up. The foliage is very good, silvery grey-blue and deeply lobed. When the stems have got as far as they want, they start to produce large, scented, papery white flowers with vivid yellow centres, which continue through late summer into autumn. Where it is happy, romneya wanders around underground, producing suckers where you may not expect them. But if that happens, consider yourself lucky. It may result in combinations better than any you had planned yourself. The catmint (*Nepeta*) can mound up its own grey foliage in between the romneya's strong stems, while a punch of yellow comes from the daylily (*Hemerocallis*). This flowers earlier in summer, and its upright, juicy foliage contrasts well with the romneya's grey elegance.

Romneya coulteri + *Nepeta racemosa* 'Walker's Low' / *Hemerocallis citrina*

① *Romneya coulteri* (White Californian tree poppy)

HEIGHT: 1–2.5 m (3–8 ft)

SPREAD: Indefinite

FLOWERING TIME: Late summer

STAR QUALITIES: Sensational flowers, with petals that seem made of crumpled white tissue paper. A lingering scent. Excellent grey foliage, irregularly divided.

ALTERNATIVES: *R.* 'White Cloud' is the variety to look for, as it has particularly glaucous foliage.

② *Nepeta racemosa* 'Walker's Low' (Catmint)

This is a more compact plant than the commonly used *N.* 'Six Hills Giant', which can easily produce stems 90 cm (36 in) long. 'Walker's Low' has a bushier habit and does not flop. The foliage is the usual catmint grey, and the hazy violet-blue flowers are produced over a long period through summer. Cut the clumps back each season to allow the new growth to come through cleanly.

③ *Hemerocallis citrina* (Daylily)

The bright, fresh foliage of bluish-green is very early into growth, a fine foil for the fragrant greenish-yellow flowers, which open towards the evening. They are less beefy than many daylilies, with long, thin petals on blooms held well above the leaves. They do not last very long, but there are plenty of them, perhaps thirty produced in succession on each stem.

1

2

3

Thalictrums, like monkshoods, make superb garden plants, because their foliage is almost as good as their flowers. Above a robust mound of grey-green leaves, 'Hewitt's Double' bears a haze of tiny mauve flowers that, because they are sterile, last an unusually long time through the second half of summer. Molinia, the purple moor grass, will get taller than the thalictrum, so is best used as a backdrop where its tall, arching sprays of purplish-green flower heads can drop down between the stands of thalictrum. Both will do best in dampish ground, where they can be joined by a burst of spring excitement from 'Thalia' or some other pale narcissus planted in the ground between the two perennials. Thalictrums do not start into growth until quite late in spring, and 'Hewitt's Double' can be slow to establish; it is well worth the wait.

Thalictrum delavayi 'Hewitt's Double' + *Molinia caerulea* subsp. *arundinacea* 'Windspiel' / *Narcissus* 'Thalia'

(1) *Thalictrum delavayi* 'Hewitt's Double'

HEIGHT: 1.5 m (5 ft)

SPREAD: 60 cm (24 in)

FLOWERING TIME: High summer

STAR QUALITIES: Excellent finely cut foliage. Unusually long-lasting sprays of fluffy mauve flowers.

ALTERNATIVES: *T. aquilegifolium* and its splendid dark-flowered variety 'Thundercloud' will flower earlier than *T. delavayi*; 'Black Stockings' has masses of lavender-coloured flowers held on striking black stems.

(2) *Molinia caerulea* subsp. *arundinacea* 'Windspiel' (Purple moor grass)

An elegant, late-flowering grass with airy, wide-spaced flower heads. It grows like a herbaceous perennial, dying down in winter, with young leaves emerging in spring from yellowish shoots that turn green as they develop. In flower, they have a carefree, almost diaphanous quality, with arched stems ending in beaded, purple-green seed heads.

(3) *Narcissus* 'Thalia'

N. 'Thalia' has no scent, a fault that needs to be acknowledged immediately. But the colour is so good and the habit so engaging that you forgive it this glaring oversight. It grows about 38 cm (15 in) high, with two or three small, creamy white flowers on a stem. Each has narrow, pointed petals and a relatively shallow, frilly cup. It flowers in mid-spring.

1

2

3

Seeming almost to engulf this stone-flagged path at Gravetye Manor in Sussex, UK, a glorious jostle of plants includes tall verbascum, the larkspur 'Sublime Azure Blue' and the feathery, tactile fronds of *Stipa tenuissima*.

IV

Into Autumn

The warm, still days of autumn often provide the best gardening conditions of the year. The soil has become moist again, but not so wet that it cannot easily be worked. The ground is still warm and the air too, and dahlias and other autumn flowers are bursting with new blooms ripe for cutting. There is an element of chance about these gorgeous days of autumn: each one, you feel, might be the last, and nothing can be taken for granted. This might be the last day you see golden leaves hanging from your little Japanese maple. This might be the last chance to sniff up the swoony scent from the long trumpet of a white tobacco flower (*Nicotiana sylvestris*; see p.144) before frost cuts it down to the ground in a crumpled, blackened heap.

In smallish gardens, it is not worth planting too many things that have nothing to say after their brief autumn speech. What you need are performers that can provide a splendid sculptural presence through the dark days of winter ahead, or produce a spring or summer act as good as their autumn one. In this respect, the autumn-flowering cyclamen (*Cyclamen hederifolium*; see p.174) is astounding. It has a long season, no vices and grows well in places that other plants would not like. The flowers (pink or white) come before the leaves, and though they seem fragile, they emerge undeterred in late summer and continue until late autumn. They have the appealing quality of small creatures heading into a gale that is too strong for them.

Autumn cyclamen do not shout at you, but it is odd how once you have got them in the garden, you find excuses to go and see how they are doing. Part of their charm is that they are always doing well. Pests and diseases pass them by. The beautiful marbled leaves emerge with the last of the flowers and have an innate ability to hold themselves well and arrange themselves thoughtfully in a clump, giving all an equal opportunity to display their intricate paintwork. They will still be looking good when spring bulbs start to come up among them.

What you are mostly looking for in the autumn garden are things that speak of the season, with lovely leaves, flowers or fruit, but which pay rent at other times of the year too. You may have a general perception of the scene as gold and yellow and red and brown, a kilim carpet laid on the earth. But if you choose to, you can bring in flashes of blue and purple as well, perhaps using tall *Verbena bonariensis* (see p.180) or the extraordinary purple bead berries of a shrub such as *Callicarpa bodinieri* under your tree of autumn gold. The cyclamen can add a sweep of pink and white, spreading under the shrub.

Using just those few elements together – tree, shrub and groundcover – you have a distillation of the autumn garden, but with elements in each that will carry through into other seasons too. In a small garden, the tree will be the most important choice. Maple provides beautiful leaves; crab apple, thorn and rowan (*Sorbus aucuparia*) will give you the bonus of good fruit as well. Maples and thorns grow very slowly, while crab apples and rowans, as well as other members of the sorbus family such as *Sorbus* 'Embley' (clusters of gorgeous orange-red fruit), *S. vilmorinii* (pink berries) and *S. cashmiriana* (ghostly white berries), grow faster, but not too fast.

Autumn is by far the best time to plant trees and shrubs. If you plant in spring, the roots have no time to establish themselves before they have to send up food and drink to the new leaves and flowers emerging above ground. The plant gets stressed, and unless it is given plenty of help – water and a thick mulch of nutritious compost – may decide to give up the struggle. A shrub planted after leaf-drop in autumn has only to think about its roots, and those will go on growing until the end of the year. By the time it wakes up again in spring, its roots will be well settled in their surroundings and able to supply what is needed.

Though you may not garden in autumn with the same driven fervour you do in spring, it is a waste to put the place to bed too early in the year. You could be enjoying liriope, autumn crocus (see p.182) and yellow sternbergia. You could be experimenting with new fuchsias. You could be gambling with agapanthus. Don't miss out on two extra months of gardening. With frost hovering in the wings, each fresh bud that appears seems a hostage to fortune. Would your star plant perhaps be a dahlia? If you have always been frightened by dahlias, acclimatize yourself gradually by growing a strain of the fine species *D. coccinea*, with its single, chalky red flowers held on wide, airy stems. The whole plant is less hefty and congested than a hybrid. Or perhaps, as your favourite, you might choose *Canna* × *ehemanii*, with its vast, paddle-shaped leaves that unfurl gradually from high summer. The startling magenta flowers come later, held in elegant, drooping panicles that are unlike most other cannas, which flower on stiff, upright spikes. Both the dahlia and canna are late starting into growth, so to get the most out of your garden, you might need to arrange an ephemeral display of spring bulbs to cover the ground while these two get going. In cold areas, both will have been lifted from the ground and stored under cover for winter. In milder areas, the tubers may overwinter in the ground under an eiderdown of dry leaves.

Dahlias and cannas are very leafy, but when their flowers emerge, they are uncompromising in colour. If you are planting them with companions that flower at the same time, think deep red, deep blue, purple, magenta, pink, cream and buff. All those shades will blend happily with them. But given their late start, you may choose instead a plant that peaks at an entirely different season, perhaps the fine old double peony, *P. officinalis* 'Rubra Plena'. Or you could build on the leafy theme, aiming for a subtropical, almost jungly look with plumes of royal fern (*Osmunda regalis*; see p.78), rough hands of rodgersia with buff flowers, the great crinkled cabbage leaves of crambe, fronds of generous *Geranium palmatum* or scimitar-shaped fans of crinum, whose trumpet flowers will join those of the dahlia and canna in late summer.

Purple-leaved bugbane (*Actaea simplex* 'Atropurpurea') is another possibility, a beautiful plant that will grow up to 1.2 m (4 ft), the leaves elegantly lobed and cut. It flowers in late autumn, with long, thin, creamy spikes, and like the crinum coincides with the dahlia and the canna. Though the crinum's flowers are far showier, the bugbane has the advantage of better foliage, saturated in deep colour and well-made enough to provide a feature on its own earlier in the season. Also purple-bronze is the sedum *Hylotelephium* 'Lynda Windsor', which is one of the tall kinds, with clusters of deep reddish-purple flowers. Like the bugbanes, the sedums are useful performers at a time when most of the garden is winding down. If you wanted more lightness and movement in the group, you might choose a grass such as *Pennisetum macrourum*, a clumping, evergreen plant that has flower spikelets that look like caterpillars hanging off the end of its stems in autumn. They start pale creamy green and turn purple and brown as they age. The grass would have the advantage of leavening the heavier foliage of dahlia or canna, especially the canna. Purple coneflowers (*Echinacea purpurea*) would be another possibility, though the foliage is coarse – perhaps too coarse to put with canna or dahlia.

If you want to keep your options open, you might choose less permanent plantings. You could join up clumps of sweet william with groups of a dark-flowered snapdragon (*Antirrhinum majus*) such as 'Ruby' – not one of the dwarfed varieties, but a sensible snapdragon: 'Ruby' is 90 cm (36 in) in height. Sometimes both sweet williams and snapdragons hang on as short-lived perennials and consequently come into flower much earlier than plants raised from seed. Then their flowering will not coincide with either the dahlia or the canna. But if you cut off the main spike of a snapdragon after it has flowered, lesser spikelets will then flower on much later into autumn. For a deep red snapdragon, to put perhaps alongside *Canna iridiflora* and the elegant grass *Pennisetum macrourum*, try 'Black Prince', which has dark, velvety, dark red flowers over foliage that is slightly bronzed.

Dramatic late summer effects can be created in the garden using nothing but annuals, exploiting their capacity to flower late and encouraging them to take over from earlier flowering perennials. There is a huge range of colours available from annual flowers. That is a blessing, of course, but it also calls for forethought on the part of the gardener. The best effects will arise from having a particular colour scheme in mind. It might be yellow, which can blaze away in the company of the oranges and bronzes that come from rudbeckias and heleniums. Teamed with lime-green and white, yellow will become cooler, more classical. Either combination could contain enormous sunflowers, with heads big enough to knock you out should they happen to fall your way.

If you go for the cool effect, lime-green nicotiana will be one of your stalwarts, growing at its proper height rather than in a dwarfed state. White cosmos will be another, the clean simple flowers set against surprisingly good foliage. There are not many annuals noted for their leaves. Both these flowers are easy to raise from seed and go together well, the tobacco flower's stodgy foliage relieved by the featheriness of the other. Try them with tall, acid-yellow African marigolds, then lace the whole lot together with creeping tendrils of lime-green helichrysum.

Alternatively, the white in this kind of scheme might come from frilly petunias and snapdragons, planted again with the lime-green nicotianas and *Cosmos sulphureus* 'Bright Lights'. Cosmos flower over an extraordinarily long season, and this mixture has flowers in yellows and oranges, both single and double. If you prefer single colours, *C.* 'Xanthos' is a soft, pale yellow, compact (60 cm / 24 in) and wonderful for cutting. You could try grey helichrysum instead of the lime-green one, letting it bob up among yellow snapdragons and seed-raised bedding dahlias. Underplant tall yellow and white zinnias with alyssum and the pretty little white-flowered *Nierembergia* 'Mont Blanc'. Each of these combinations sticks to the same yellow, lime-green and white theme, but each will give subtly different results. Try different combinations either side of the same path: mirror planting, but swerving enough to be interesting.

The way you approach autumn in the garden depends very much on your character and state of mind. You may by this stage be itching to cut everything down, clear everything away and start thinking about something else. Or you may want to continue gardening as vividly, joyously and dangerously as you do for the rest of the year – in which case, you will delight in the notion that you can gallop into autumn surrounded by blazing dahlias, forests of zinnias, jungly cannas and banana palms. Instead of watching a traditional herbaceous border quietly falling apart at the seams, you can have explosions of pampas grass and sunflowers, and eruptions of zinnias and dahlias, which by now will be at the top of their form. If you want it to, your garden can look as rich and profligate in late summer and autumn as it does in late spring. After all, there are kniphofias, such as orange-red *K. rooperi*, that have not even begun to flower yet.

Try plunging pots of sweet smelling acidantheras among coleus and pale grey succulents with leaves the shape of cow's tongues. Mix with them the tall blue flowering spikes of *Salvia farinacea* and elegant umbels of tulbaghia. Where has tulbaghia been all my life, you may ask when you first see it. It resembles an allium, but of lighter build, the flowers pinkish-mauve, the heads smaller than those of most alliums. Make a virtue of the fact that autumn's colours are fire colours by planting dahlias such as the orange 'Ellen Huston', setting the blazing colour against the dark, sulky foliage of castor oil plants (see p.186). Use the glowing 'Orange Mullet' dahlia with the tender Bhutan ginger *Hedychium greenei*. Try the rich pink dahlia 'Pearl of Heemstede' against the velvety Mexican salvia, *S. involucrata* 'Bethellii'. If that is too pink for you, tone the group down with dark blue-flowered *Lycianthes rantonnetii*, the kind of thing you might normally think of using in a conservatory. Live dangerously. Experiment with other plants such as papyrus and begonia, which you may be more used to thinking of as house plants. It is extraordinary what they can do when given their heads outside, at least until the first frost comes.

Autumn Annuals

Annual flowers provide the icing on the cake of the garden, and there is no reason to deny yourself the pleasure of having them alongside other, more sustaining ingredients. Though your cake recipe may stay roughly the same each year, you can experiment with different trimmings. There is no quicker way to change the look of a garden than by planting annuals; not the same ones each year, but different plants in different colours, set in different places. Some peak in high summer and have run out by late summer, but many are slower to get into top gear and are at their best as summer drifts into autumn.

Any garden centre can supply a standard palette of annuals: French marigolds, lobelia, geraniums, petunias, busy lizzies. But after running through all these permutations (remembering that these are standards because they are reliable, tough survivors), any gardener with an ounce of curiosity wants to experiment with plants that the garden centre does not provide. Beware, though, of that favourite seed catalogue word, 'distinctive'. It is a sign of desperation on the part of the seed merchant. Increasingly too, you find 'dwarf' put forward as a virtue. Why is it a good thing to stick eleven dwarf plants into a space that five decent-sized ones could occupy more elegantly? As we are not getting any closer to the ground ourselves, dwarfing plants is a perverse trend.

Placing is important, with annuals as with any other kind of plant in the garden. It is no good raising plants if you do not then show them off to best advantage. First, you have to put the plants where they are most likely to thrive. Generally, annuals do better in sun than shade (though that is not true of non-stop begonias or busy lizzies). Then they need friendly neighbours that will complement them in colour and form and not overwhelm them in terms of size.

Sometimes you might make groups entirely of annuals, although they generally look best combined with more permanent features. Take a cordyline, for instance – a handsome plant by any criterion. If you pack deep purple heliotrope and deep pink ivy-leaved geraniums round its feet, it begins to look more generous (and interesting). The vanilla scent of heliotrope is reason enough to grow it, but the foliage is dramatic too: deep green with a purplish flush, the leaves furrowed by their network of veins.

Top: In a private English garden in Radcot, Oxfordshire, *Verbena bonariensis* provides a light screen in front of *Helianthus* 'Lemon Queen' and *Symphyotrichum novae-angliae* 'Rosa Sieger'.

Above: Zinnias come into their own in late summer and will continue to blaze away until cut down by the first frost. Ever useful *Verbena bonariensis* has stems slender enough to push through other plants without hurting them.

Like geraniums, the best kinds are perennials used as annuals; you can keep them going with cuttings. Try it with tall, willowy, purple *Verbena bonariensis* (see p.180) and dark purple kale, *Brassica oleracea* 'Ragged Jack', which is much too handsome to bury in the vegetable patch.

Sunflowers (*Helianthus*) could easily be the stars of a quick-fix garden, peaking late in the season, when they could rise out of a sea of nasturtiums and lord it over dahlias in the same range of colours. They are at their best in late summer and have become as desirable as the rarest salvia ever was, but so much easier. Nor do they take themselves as seriously: nothing is as effective at lightening the urban jungle. Sow them in late spring, setting each seed in a 7.5 cm (3 in) pot. Watered well, then wrapped in clingfilm, the pots should need no attention until the seedlings poke through. The plants can go outside in late spring, when all danger of frost has passed. Sunflowers generally take four months to start flowering from seed, so if you sow early, they will peak early. *H.* 'Claret' is a beauty, with mahogany petals set around dark centres. Try it with cannas and among tall stands of miscanthus or stipa. It will easily reach 1.5 m (5 ft).

Because sunflowers have become so fashionable as cut flowers, the bonus for gardeners is that there are now masses of different kinds to choose from. Colours range upwards and downwards from the standard bright yellow to include a pale ivory and a deep, rich mahogany. *Helianthus* 'Moonshine', for instance, is a branching type about 1.5 m (5 ft) tall, with pale yellow petals around dark, velvety centres. 'Valentine' produces long-stemmed flowers, wonderful to cut, of a soft lemon-yellow, while 'Italian White' branches out to make a splendid show of creamy white flowers.

Sunflowers have been planted in English cottage gardens for so long, they seem part of the scenery, but like so many English garden flowers, they are, in fact, foreigners. Brought over from America in the sixteenth century, English gardeners first learned about them in *Joyfull Newes out of the Newe Founde Worlde*, originally published in Spanish and translated in 1577 by the super-optimist John Frampton. 'It casteth out the greatest flowers', he wrote, 'and the moste perticulars that ever hath been seen, for it is greater than a great Platter or Dishe, the whiche hath divers coulers ... It showeth marveilous faire in Gardines.'

From the same part of the world at about the same time came the nasturtium, which you can also start off in pots for a late summer garden. *Tropaeolum majus* 'Jewel of Africa' has long trailing shoots of marbled foliage. 'Empress of India' is much bushier, with steely blue-green leaves and luscious, deep red flowers (see p.124). Nasturtiums are a gamble. Sometimes they get choked with blackfly, but unmolested, they quickly spread to make a weed-suppressing mat of colour under other plants. They may even try to climb up the sunflowers' stems – which, thankfully, are strong enough to take on such assaults.

California poppies, nasturtiums and pot marigolds are all reliable staples. They are easy, cheerful flowers, and you need a few stalwarts you can depend on among sometimes traitorous novelties. They are good flowers to use in mixes with vegetables too: California poppies with frizzy endive or lettuce, nasturtiums to make a carpet under standard gooseberries, pot marigolds to jazz up a planting of spinach. You could also try planting sunflowers among your sweetcorn.

Shrubs for Structure

Furnishing a garden is rather like furnishing a room. It is best to start with the bigger things – the sofa, the armchairs – and get them in place before scattering around cushions and books. Shrubs are the outside equivalent of the sofas and chairs. When you have good shrubs in place, providing interest for as many months in the year as possible, then you can start filling in with bulbs, perennials and annuals. But which shrubs? That depends on the type of garden you have. Is it mostly sunny, or shady? How tough are your winters? What shelter can you offer against wind? Is the ground light or heavy? Is the soil acid or neutral? If you have acid soil, you can wallow in camellias, rhododendrons and magnolias. If not, not.

Ever since plantsmen started bringing strange exotics into this country, gardeners have enjoyed the risk of growing them. If the gamble comes off, you feel inordinately proud. If it does not, well, there's always another season, another good reason to kid yourself that this time everything will be different. The hazards usually have to do with hardiness. Myrtle (*Myrtus communis*) is a superb shrub that flowers from late summer into autumn, desirable for its foliage, flowers, scent, bark, everything. Wherever you check though, you will find it marked as not reliably hardy. But the number of old cottages in English villages bearing the name of an ancient myrtle now propping up the porch suggests that it is a long-established favourite and, with a little thought, worth the gamble. Sometimes the shelter of a south or west wall is the answer. The evergreen foliage is neat, dark and spicily aromatic, and the flowers come at the end of summer just when we need fresh treats. Bees love them, rolling around in the powder puff of stamens at the centre of each small white flower. Given a sheltered position, myrtle will bloom for at least two months, the flowers followed by small black fruits. It is a Mediterranean native, and the fruit, though not showy like that of the cotoneaster, is curiously elegant and appealing. If you are looking for a filler to set off flowers in a jug inside, you can scarcely do better than sprigs of myrtle in early autumn, with its dark green leaves punctuated by equally neat, dark berries.

You need a good proportion of evergreen shrubs in the garden, not only to furnish it in winter but also to provide a background for summer annuals and bulbs. Invaluable evergreenery comes from shrubby spurges such as *Euphorbia mellifera* and *Euphorbia* × *pasteurii*. You may have planted them for their late spring flowers, greenish-yellow and honey-scented in the case of *E. mellifera*. But their bulk, their splendid luminous green presence, is there for all seasons. Because so much else in the garden dives underground in preparation for winter, we notice them more in this late season than any other. The honey spurge has the useful habit of producing a constant supply of new shoots from the base. Eventually it builds into a handsome, rounded bush about 1.5 m (5 ft) high and wide. The fleshy stems are clothed with oblong leaves, each with a distinct white midrib. By this time in late summer, its heads of stiff, tawny-coloured flowers have come and gone, but the structure of this spurge and its fleshy foliage remain important markers in the garden. The shrubby hare's ear (*Bupleurum fruticosum*) has the same attributes. It is not as showy, but not everything in the garden should shout. Its evergreen foliage is darker than the spurges' and provides a splendid setting for the stiff umbels of small, acid-yellow flowers in late summer. That may be its particular season, but it stands, a handsome landmark, all year, while foxgloves and acidanthera, ammi and verbena come and go around it.

Hydrangeas with Style

By late summer, hydrangeas come into their own, and though few are evergreen, some (*H. quercifolia*, for instance) have splendid foliage, which is as much of a gift in a garden as the big heads of flowers. The lacecap types have flattish heads with dense, nubby centres made up of masses of tiny flowers, each head surrounded by an airy circlet of things that look like petals but are not. There is a splendid grace and easiness in company about lacecaps, such as the superlative *H.* 'Mariesii Perfecta' ('Blue Wave'). But the mopheads (also known as Hortensias) have punch, and if you want a hydrangea for a tub to catch the eye, then a mophead such as the rich crimson 'Merveille Sanguine' or the elegant white 'Soeur Therese' might be just the thing. Make it a big tub, and never let it dry out.

Although, to a gardener, the mopheads and lacecaps seem so different, they are all lumped together in the same huge group, *H. macrophylla*. Flowers will be pinkish or bluish depending on the soil. For true blue you need acid soil, with plenty of aluminium in it. Gardeners, desperate for blue but with the wrong kind of soil, may try doses of a bluing agent, but in the long run, it is best to go with the flow and accept what the plant can naturally do. The good news for those with shady gardens is that hydrangeas love shade. They will grow in sun, but by nature they are woodlanders, growing more lush and luscious in shade. In shade, a white-flowered hydrangea such as *H. macrophylla* 'Veitchii' will glimmer with a luminosity you do not get with pink or blue-flowered types. Try it with deep blue monkshood, and fill in round its feet with the Japanese painted fern (*Athyrium niponicum*). Hydrangeas are long-lived shrubs, so start them off well. Town gardens, especially, often have hungry soils, which can be helped by adding mulch.

On a shady bank you could try several white-flowered lacecaps – *H.* 'Mariesii Grandiflora', 'Grant's Choice' or 'Lanarth White' (see p.178). All are superb. The underplanting might include treats for the earlier part of the year: plenty of snowdrops for spring, small-leaved variegated periwinkle and white-flowered woodruff to keep weeds at bay, a few clumps of epimedium for contrast. White-flowered foxgloves would fit in well too, making tall spires between the mounded humps of the shrubs. Growing conditions will determine the ultimate size of hydrangeas such as these, but you can generally expect them to hover around 1.2–1.5 m (4–5 ft), becoming as wide as they are high.

Hydrangeas belonging to the *H. macrophylla* group are perhaps the ones most commonly seen in gardens, but there are other beauties, particularly those found in the *H. aspera* group. There are several distinct types, including the Villosas and the Sargentianas, both of which come from China. *Hydrangea aspera* subsp. *sargentiana* (see p.142) stars in the High Summer section of this book. The Villosas flower later, with leaves that are long and narrow, hairy, but softer to the touch than those of Sargent's hydrangea. The flower heads last a very long time. They are quite deep in tone, with a central mass of tiny flowers surrounded by a ring of much bigger, but sterile florets. The overall impression is a blur of deep mauve.

Hydrangeas of the Villosa type have a loose, relaxed habit and are very generous with their flowers. They have the natural elegance that few man-made crosses can achieve. In a garden that has space for them, they look more at home than hydrangeas such as *H. paniculata* 'Limelight'. The Paniculatas carry their flowers in big, broad cones, which in 'Limelight' are a greenish kind of white. It is a fine plant, but hard pruned, as it often is, the flower heads seem almost too big, out of scale with the shrub on which they are growing. They draw too much attention to themselves, which can upset the balance of a garden. Nevertheless, they can be stars in a particular kind of pared-down, shady town garden of good paving, topiary and tubs. *H. arborescens* 'Annabelle' would be equally at home here, with huge rounded heads of white flowers.

Unexpected Delights

Autumn often brings unexpected guests. You might be able to watch a scarlet oriental poppy unfold itself from its green pod, shaking out its silk petals as you might a shirt that has been packed too long in a suitcase. This is a flower of early summer, but given the right conditions it sometimes puts on a wild late performance. It is only one of the perennials that finds the mild, damp weather that sometimes comes in late autumn a rather better growing proposition than early summer, the appointment we had made for it in our own rather more rigid diaries. Delphiniums often throw up late flowering spikes too, shorter than the summer ones, but strange and welcome interlopers in an autumn melange that may be predominantly painted in shades of orange, russet and brown. Or you may get spring flowers leaping early onto the canvas – primroses, perhaps, or double daisies (*Bellis perennis*) with powder puff flowers sitting fatly on rosettes of fleshy leaves.

The effect is of a shambolic army, the troops all marching to different tunes. Only a few stalwarts are proceeding at the pace we expect. Some divisions that should be bringing up the rear are overtaking the leaders. Some that we thought had shot their bolt have regrouped and charged in with new ammunition. It might be a general's nightmare, but for gardeners it can be glorious – provided you do not mind throwing away the rule book. The message? Enjoy. The show may close any day now, when winter arrives in earnest.

Mild conditions at this late season are a boon to all kinds of tender perennials such as the salvia family and the various types of osteospermum and argyranthemum. These opportunists will be joined by other flowers that can quite properly claim late autumn as their own season. Such is the old cottage garden chrysanthemum called 'Emperor of China', a reliably perennial chrysanthemum with soft, dirty pink flowers. The first petals are quilled, opening out to flat spoon shapes at the extremities. The centre part of the flower, then in bud, makes a dark contrast with the paler pink of the opened petals. As the flower ages, the quill effect disappears, and you end up with a pale, fully double flower, spicily scented. A proper frost turns the leaves rich crimson, when it becomes even showier. Try it with plum-coloured *Salvia* 'Nachtvlinder' and flowery umbels of nerine. When they have died down, it will almost be time to start looking for the first signs of winter aconites. The best gardens never have a metaphorical CLOSED sign on the gate.

Top: Pale flower heads of *Hydrangea arborescens* 'Annabelle' dominate this planting at Winson Manor, near Cirencester in Gloucestershire, UK. Planted alongside are clumps of dark *Salvia nemorosa* 'Caradonna' and the long-flowering *Geranium* 'Johnson's Blue'.

Above: Deep pink tassels of *Persicaria orientalis* dangle in front of a bold clump of *Miscanthus sinensis* 'Morning Light', with *Salvia* 'Indigo Spires' in the foreground.

The splendid, witchy monkshood has a faintly sinister air about it. Take note of that, for it is extremely poisonous, though that is no reason not to grow it. The flowers are of the deep, intense blue we associate with delphiniums, but they are easier to grow and not so prone to slug damage. They will be happiest in cool, moist, fertile soil with some shade, but they will grow happily in full sun, provided the soil is not starved and dry. The extraordinary scarlet and orange fruits of the shrubby spindle (*Euonymus planipes*) will provide a dramatic background, and its leaves will add to the show as autumn advances, turning a brilliant red. The fennel (*Ferula communis*) produces an invaluable fountain of brilliant, ferny foliage in the improbable months at the beginning of the year – a superb foil for spring bulbs.

Aconitum carmichaelii 'Arendsii' + *Ferula communis* / *Euonymus planipes* 'Sancho'

① *Aconitum carmichaelii* 'Arendsii' (Monkshood)

HEIGHT: 1.2 m (4 ft)

SPREAD: 30 cm (12 in)

FLOWERING TIME: Early autumn

STAR QUALITIES: Flowers of a most intense blue, borne in branched heads. Strong growth habit. Excellent in cool, moist shade.

ALTERNATIVES: *A.* 'Bressingham Spire' (see p.140) has stems up to 90 cm (36 in) clothed in deep violet flowers; *A.* × *cammarum* 'Bicolor' has pale blue flowers washed over with whitish-grey; 'Kelmscott' has tall panicles of lavender-blue flowers.

② *Ferula communis* (Giant fennel)

This is a completely different animal to the edible fennel (*Foeniculum vulgare*). Its main use is as a foliage plant, for though the flowering stem is dramatically vast – up to 5 m (15 ft) high – the plant often dies after flowering. But during the years that it is building up to this apocalyptic last act, it produces fountains of fresh foliage very early in the year. The green is of an unnatural brilliance, and the foliage is even more dense and feathery than its edible cousin's. It is a glorious thing.

③ *Euonymus planipes* 'Sancho' (Spindle)

This spindle has long, pointed buds breaking out into the inconspicuous greenish flowers that produce the astounding fruit. They hang on long stalks in little clusters, each one made up of four segments, like the overstuffed divisions of a pumpkin. When these bright pink-red cases split, they show the brilliant orange seed covering inside. This particular species comes from northeast China and the far east of Russia, but it is a widespread group, tough and easy. 'Sancho' makes an upright shrub eventually reaching about 3 m (10 ft) and is extravagantly free flowering. The leaves turn a brilliant red in autumn, but the fruit often hang on long after the leaves have fallen.

2

3

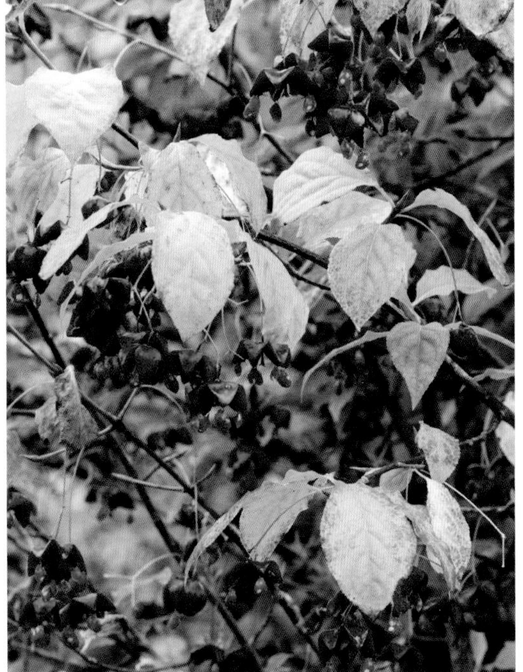

Each of these plants has great staying power. They unfold their acts slowly, but even before the flowers start to unwrap themselves you will be able to feast on the foliage. They could scarcely be more different, the dark mounds of actaea leaves contrasting with the much airier, paler foliage of the achillea. The agapanthus's strappy leaves are no more than leafish, but entirely different in form, and its blue flower spikes will sing out dramatically against the actaea, a thick, drenched combination of colours. With the pale yellow of the achillea, the blue will make a much clearer, cleaner contrast. Actaeas are easy in moist, well-fed soil but resent being poked about by over-zealous gardeners. Cut down the flowered stems in late autumn, and mulch the plants well in early spring. They do not require much more.

Actaea simplex 'Brunette' + *Agapanthus* 'Flower of Love' / *Achillea* 'Credo'

(1) *Actaea simplex* 'Brunette' (Bugbane)

HEIGHT: 1–1.2 m (3–4 ft)

SPREAD: 60 cm (24 in)

FLOWERING TIME: Early to mid-autumn

STAR QUALITIES: Splendid foliage, wine dark and deeply saturated; narrow bottle-brush flowers of cream tinged with purple.

ALTERNATIVES: *A.* 'Elstead Variety' is one of the latest into flower, with dark green leaves and purplish buds opening to creamy white flowers; *A. racemosa* (black snake root) has dark green leaves with tall spikes of creamy white flowers.

(2) *Agapanthus* 'Flower of Love'

This opens from dark buds into a mid-blue flower on stems about 40 cm (16 in) tall. For a paler grouping, use a more softly coloured variety, such as 'Windsor Grey'. At 75 cm (30 in) this is a good deal taller, though, and will not sit as comfortably in front of the actaea. 'Flower of Love' is deciduous, and there is some merit in that. You can use the space around the crown for some early flowering narcissus or scillas to capture the spring months.

(3) *Achillea* 'Credo'

Mounds of feathery grey-green foliage support big flat heads of clear, light, very pale yellow. Raised by the great twentieth century plantsman Ernst Pagels in Germany, it is a neat plant, rarely reaching more than 60 cm (24 in) in any direction, but the flowering stems may need discreet propping with twigs of hazel. Achilleas last a long time in flower, starting in early summer and continuing until autumn.

1

2

3

Few good perennials are as easy going as Japanese anemones. They are stayers too: in old, abandoned gardens where brambles and couch grass have smothered all other plants, you still see them flowering profusely (often alongside old-fashioned double red peonies), repelling all boarders, defending their territory. The foliage, tough vine-like leaves of a dull matt green, is quite late to appear, but from late summer onwards there is an astonishing succession of flowers, charmingly simple in outline, the petals gathered round a central, greenish knob. The cosmos will probably beat the anemones into flower (it depends on when they were planted out and how warm the summer has been). If sowing seed does not appeal, buy plug plants and grow them on. 'Rubenza' is a rich, dark red, wonderful to pick and incredibly generous with its flowers. The tall coppery spires of the eremurus will come before the anemone and the cosmos, an eye-catching prelude to the late summer display.

Anemone × *hybrida* 'Honorine Jobert'	+	*Eremurus* × *isabellinus* 'Cleopatra' / *Cosmos bipinnatus* 'Rubenza'

① *Anemone* × *hybrida* 'Honorine Jobert' (Japanese anemone)

HEIGHT: 1.2–1.5 m (4–5 ft)

SPREAD: 45 cm (18 in)

FLOWERING TIME: Late summer to mid-autumn

STAR QUALITIES: Strong stems do not need staking. Pure white flowers carried over a long season.

ALTERNATIVES: *A.* 'Géante des Blanches' has semi-double flowers, washed over with green on the reverse; 'Königin Charlotte' has large, semi-double, pink flowers; *A. hupehensis* 'Hadspen Abundance' is shorter (90 cm / 36 in) and has single flowers of dark pink.

② *Eremurus* × *isabellinus* 'Cleopatra' (Foxtail lily)

The fleshy roots of this magnificent plant radiate out from the crown like the spokes of a wheel. They need to be planted carefully in well-drained ground. Lax clumps of strap-shaped leaves die away in early summer as the huge flowering stems are produced. The spires are thickly set with hundreds of small, star-shaped flowers that open from the bottom of the spike upwards to make eye-catching columns. 'Cleopatra' is a beautiful coppery orange, but there are white, pink, yellow and apricot forms as well.

③ *Cosmos bipinnatus* 'Rubenza'

The cosmos take time to build up to full flowering strength, so are often at their best in an early autumn garden. 'Rubenza' stops at about 60 cm (24 in), so should not need staking. If you want something taller in that same deep, rich red, try 'Dazzler' (90 cm / 36 in); either will be a good match for the anemone. Avoid plain white varieties, which will not provide enough of a contrast. Annual cosmos plants have become great favourites because they are so profligate with their flowers – superb for cutting. There is a charming type called 'Double Click Cranberries', with petals rolled round like ice cream cones.

1

3

2

There are a few very choice, very well-mannered plants that you can never have too many of, and *Cyclamen hederifolium* is one of them. It has absolutely no vices, and the great virtue of growing in places that other, less desirable plants would spurn. Pests and diseases pass it by. You can settle it between the exposed roots of a big tree. You can grow it in quite deep shade. You can use it to make a late-flowering carpet under earlier flowering shrubs. It puts itself away neatly at the end of its growing season, leaving only its mad seed pods, the size, shape and colour of aniseed balls, to remind you of its presence. The flowers come before the leaves, poking with surprising determination through the soil in late summer and continuing till late autumn. The ivy-shaped, marbled leaves start to emerge with the last of the flowers, each leaf marbled in a pattern that is regular but slightly different on every leaf, the dark greyish-green imprinted with silver and paler shades of green. As the underground tuber gets bigger (they can get to the size of dinner plates), more and more leaves are produced, so you end with a sizeable clump. But however many there are, the pattern on each is subtly different. This fragile-looking little cyclamen takes the worst that winter can throw at it, and if you are lucky will spread to make a carpet under shrubs such as daphne and hoheria. The leaves will still be looking good when the dainty new fronds of the fern begin to uncurl. The superb, unearthly arisaema is late to emerge but will produce its extraordinary flowering cowl alongside the cyclamen.

Cyclamen hederifolium + *Arisaema ciliatum* var. *liubaense* / *Adiantum aleuticum*

① *Cyclamen hederifolium*

HEIGHT: 10–13 cm (4–5 in)

SPREAD: 15 cm (6 in)

FLOWERING TIME: Late summer to late autumn

STAR QUALITIES: Enchanting shuttlecock flowers in various shades of pink, and there is also a lovely pure white. Long-lasting leaves, roughly triangular in outline and fabulously marbled with silver.

ALTERNATIVES: No other autumn-flowering cyclamen is as easy and valuable as *C. hederifolium*; *C. coum* (see p.24) is good but flowers in spring; *C. purpurascens* has carmine-red flowers in mid- to late summer, but they are not truly hardy.

② *Arisaema ciliatum* var. *liubaense*

This arisaema is an exaggerated, much more dramatic version of the British native cuckoo pint (*Arum maculatum*), with a dramatic hooded spathe protecting a thin spadix inside. In this species the handsome foliage is arranged in a cartwheel of dark leaflets on top of a stem about 90 cm (36 in) tall. The tall, thin spadix is a rich toffee-brown spectacularly striped in white; curious ears swell under the hood, which curves protectively over the spadix. It is an astonishing creature, faintly sinister, fabulously seductive. In autumn it produces a dense stalk of brilliant red berries.

③ *Adiantum aleuticum* (Maidenhair fern)

Use this deciduous or semi-evergreen fern with anything. It stands about 30 cm (12 in) high, with long, thin, stiff fronds held almost horizontal and finely fringed. The young fronds are a pinkish sort of copper, drifting into pale green as they age. It is excellent with cyclamen and arisaemas, but big enough to group with plants such as rodgersia or scatter among the new whorls of lily stems. For much of the year, there is not a flower to be seen in groupings such as this, but the fern's slow progression through various states, always elegant, always poised, holds the stage.

2

3

There are still some sophisticates who sneer at dahlias, thinking them vulgar. Like aspidistras and giant marrows, there is a touch of the music hall about such dahlias as the dinner plate types, and even their most ardent devotees have to admit that there are some sulphurously evil yellows among the dahlia tribe. But there are plenty of others to choose from, remembering that dahlias planted all together in a random jumble do not dazzle, merely distract. Here, a graceful (yes – dahlias can be graceful) single dahlia in a rich magenta-pink with deep bronze foliage is used with salvias, the chunkiness of the dahlias offset by the shimmering plumes of the moor grass (*Molinia*). The grass may be the first plant to flower, before the dahlia and salvia get into full gear, but then there will be a generous performance until the show is brought to a crashing halt by the first frosts. Dahlias, being natives of Mexico, are tender. There is a great mystique attached to the overwintering of the tubers from which dahlias grow: the lifting, the cutting back, the dusting with flowers of sulphur, the burying in sand. It all sounds reasonable, but storing tends to be followed by the things dahlia-fanciers do not talk about: the shrivelling, the eating by mice. If you live in a reasonably mild area, you can forget the purist approach and leave the tubers in the ground, well-mulched with leaves. There are disasters associated with this course of action too – slugs and unexpectedly cold winters – but no more than the disasters that attend lifting. And you save a lot of labour.

Dahlia 'Magenta Star' + *Molinia caerulea* subsp. *arundinacea* 'Transparent' / *Salvia* 'Amistad'

---

① *Dahlia* 'Magenta Star'

HEIGHT: 1.5–1.8 m (5–6 ft)

SPREAD: 30–60 cm (12–24 in)

FLOWERING TIME: High summer to autumn

STAR QUALITIES: Brilliant panache, hot colour and dark foliage. Continues flowering until cut down by frost.

ALTERNATIVES: *D.* 'Hillcrest Royal' has spiky petals of magenta-purple swirling out from a tightly buttoned centre; 'Hamari Gold' has flowers like whirling suns; 'David Howard' has neat, rich, orange flowers set against gleaming dark bronze foliage.

② *Molinia caerulea* subsp. *arundinacea* 'Transparent' (Purple moor grass)

The common name gives the impression that the grass itself is purple, but that colour is no more than a stain at the base of the clump. The first shoots come through the ground in spring, and the stems can reach 1.8 m (6 ft). 'Transparent' arches over, though, so it never seems that tall. It is like a diaphanous fountain, the green turning to a soft butter-yellow as the season advances. Wonderfully graceful in movement and hung in early autumn with purplish beadlike seed heads.

③ *Salvia* 'Amistad'

Recent plant hunting in South America has resulted in a huge number of new salvias being introduced to lucky gardeners. 'Amistad' was bred from two species, *S. guaranitica* and *S. gesneriiflora*, and is a dramatic beauty, though unfortunately not reliably hardy. Take cuttings, just in case. From arresting black stems and calyces, lippy, silky flowers emerge in a dark bluish-purple. It is a powerful combination, especially as flowering stems can reach 1.5 m (5 ft). Bees love them, and the flowers obligingly produce a long season for foraging, from high summer right through to the first frosts. Leave the stems on through winter to provide a little protection to the subterranean crown.

3

1

2

Blues and whites predominate in this selection, ideal for a partially shaded spot in the garden. By choosing different varieties of either the geranium or the hydrangea, you can switch the emphasis and the flowering times. If it suits you to have more action earlier in the season, choose a geranium such as 'Mrs Kendall Clarke', which comes into flower in early summer. Or combine a white-flowered geranium with a deep blue hydrangea such as *H. macrophylla* 'Nachtigall'. The geranium Rozanne ('Gerwat') is a go-anywhere plant, and it advances with the solid determination of a canvassing politician. This makes it a useful thing to use, for instance, on an awkward slope. Once settled, it will clump up and flower over a long season. It is a splendid, reliable thing, voted Plant of the Centenary in 2013, when the Royal Horticultural Society celebrated a hundred years of the Chelsea Flower Show. Add a hydrangea such as 'Lanarth White' to give structure to the planting and for the pleasure of its white lacecap flowers. The hellebore has handsome evergreen foliage and offers extra delight in winter with its pale celadon-green flowers.

Geranium Rozanne ('Gerwat') + *Helleborus foetidus* / *Hydrangea macrophylla* 'Lanarth White'

(1) *Geranium* Rozanne ('Gerwat')

HEIGHT: 60 cm (24 in)

SPREAD: 80 cm (32 in)

FLOWERING TIME: High summer to autumn

STAR QUALITIES: Attractive lobed and toothed leaves. Saucer-shaped, sky-blue flowers with white centres produced over a long season. Spreads generously but does not root as it goes.

ALTERNATIVES: *G.* 'Ann Folkard' has magenta flowers with black centres; *G. wallichianum* 'Buxton's Variety' has blue flowers on trailing stems; *G. himalayense* 'Gravetye' has blue flowers over foliage that colours in autumn; *G.* 'Johnson's Blue' produces blue flowers during summer; *G.* × *magnificum* has purplish-blue flowers at mid-summer; *G. pratense* 'Mrs Kendall Clark' has stripey, blue-grey flowers on tall plants in early summer.

(2) *Helleborus foetidus* (Stinking hellebore)

If ever a plant needed a name change, this is it. It is impossible to sell itself while saddled with such a terrible tag, which is a pity, because it is a handsome thing. It holds itself well, and in winter and early spring the dark, evergreen leaves, deeply cut and fingered, are topped with pale green bundles of flower that last for months. And it does not stink at all.

(3) *Hydrangea macrophylla* 'Lanarth White'

'Lanarth White' is a reasonably compact lacecap hydrangea, slowly reaching about 1.5 m (5 ft) high and wide. The sterile florets, the showy bits of the flower head, are pure white, surrounding a centre made up of tiny flowers of blue or pink. Hydrangeas are generally bluish in an acid soil, pinkish otherwise. The hydrangea and geranium are relaxed companions, happy in a wildish part of the garden, where both will provide a long season of flowers.

2

1

3

Flowering in this group starts with a sprinkle of sweet-smelling white blooms on the variegated myrtle (*Luma*), which can be clipped to make a handsome cone against which the nerines and the verbena will shine. The variegation is gentle, the tiny leaves of greyish-green irregularly edged with cream. This shrub is a charming, slow-growing delight, though best suited to a reasonably sheltered site. A harsh frost may burn some of the foliage, but it quickly repairs itself when the weather warms up. The verbena has scarcely any foliage and thinks only of flowering, producing little bunches of them, scattered at the ends of tall, immensely thin branching stems. Although it is sometimes too enthusiastic in its self-seeding, you rarely tire of it because it is so delicate. The effect is like looking through a bead curtain at whatever lies beyond. The nerine will be the last plant to come into flower in this group and, like the luma, is not fully hardy (this species comes from South Africa). Plant them shallowly, so that the noses of the bulbs are just above ground. Like colchicums, they flower without their leaves. The strappy foliage follows later and does not die down until the following summer.

Luma apiculata 'Glanleam Gold' + *Nerine bowdenii* / *Verbena bonariensis*

(1) *Luma apiculata* 'Glanleam Gold'

HEIGHT: 3 m (10 ft)

SPREAD: 3 m (10 ft)

FLOWERING TIME: Summer to early autumn

STAR QUALITIES: Charming evergreen foliage, neatly and unaggressively variegated. A slow-growing shrub that can be left to grow freely or is easily clipped to a topiary shape. Small white flowers with showy powder puffs of stamens at their centres.

ALTERNATIVES: The common myrtle (*Myrtus communis*) is similar, but the leaves are plain dark green, and the white flowers start slightly later in the summer.

(2) *Nerine bowdenii*

On stems about 45 cm (18 in) tall, the nerine produces rounded heads of pink trumpet flowers, each like a small lily. They are late coming into flower, a rather luscious and extravagant treat when so many other garden plants are finishing. A good summer baking encourages plenty of flowers through autumn. In cold areas, mulch clumps when they have finished flowering to give extra protection against frost. They make excellent cut flowers, if you can spare them from the garden.

(3) *Verbena bonariensis*

Most perennials fuss about too long with their leaves before they even think of flowering, but *V. bonariensis* gets straight on with the job. Most of its leaves are clustered in a smallish basal rosette. From this rises the tall, thin branching stem with a constant succession of little purple flowers, pushing out from clumps at the ends of the stems. They are devoted self-seeders.

3

1

2

The common polypody is a plain fern, made up of a stiffish midrib with simple leaflets sprouting along it at regular intervals, but there are many different variations on the theme, including *P. cambricum* 'Richard Kayse', found by Mr Kayse at Dinas Powys in South Wales in 1668. That plant was sterile, and so could only be increased and spread by division. We twenty-first-century gardeners have in our hands a form that has come down to us in an unbroken line from the seventeenth century. The fronds are wider and lacier than the common polypody, a bright, fresh green, and so deeply divided as to look like lace. Most ferns unfurl their fresh fronds in late spring, but this one saves its newest clothes for late summer, pushing out its fresh fronds when other plants are beginning to look tired and dusty. It then shines all through autumn and winter. It colonizes well, the fleshy rhizomes creeping slowly across ground in sun or partial shade. It is at its best in damp, rich soil. The polypody will get along in any company but is particularly good as a background to the autumn-flowering colchicum. It dies down in mid-spring, by which time the fritillaries will be pushing through to furnish the ground. This is a relaxed, natural looking group of plants. As the splendid Cotswold nurseryman Bob Brown says, 'Ferns never look domesticated' – his nursery, set up in 1990, is a happy hunting ground for fern lovers.

Polypodium cambricum 'Richard Kayse' + *Fritillaria meleagris* / *Colchicum agrippinum*

---

(1) *Polypodium cambricum* 'Richard Kayse' (Polypody)

HEIGHT: 38–45 cm (15–18 in)

SPREAD: Indefinite

FLOWERING TIME: Evergreen fern

STAR QUALITIES: Evergreen. Excellent groundcover. New foliage appears in late summer, when fresh green leaves are most welcome.

ALTERNATIVES: *P. cambricum* 'Cristatum' has fronds with crests on the tips and at the ends of the pinnae; *P. cambricum* 'Whilharris' has slightly narrower fronds.

(2) *Fritillaria meleagris* (Snake's head fritillary)

Although now rare in the wild, these fritillaries are not difficult to establish in the garden. They do not like to be chivvied; you just have to wait while they decide whether they like you or not. If they do, they will flower in mid-spring in their bell-like, mysterious way. The flowers are chequerboards of purple, pink and white; some flowers are white, tinged with green. The leaves are thin and grassy, and the whole plant has a kind of fragile sadness that is very touching.

(3) *Colchicum agrippinum* (Autumn crocus)

The flowers leap through the ground in autumn, making elegant, long-stemmed goblets. The leaves follow much later, forming surprisingly large clumps that last until mid-summer of the following season. This species has flowers 8–10 cm (3–4 in) tall, of a deep purplish-pink, checked or tessellated with a paler colour in the way that the snake's head fritillaries are.

2

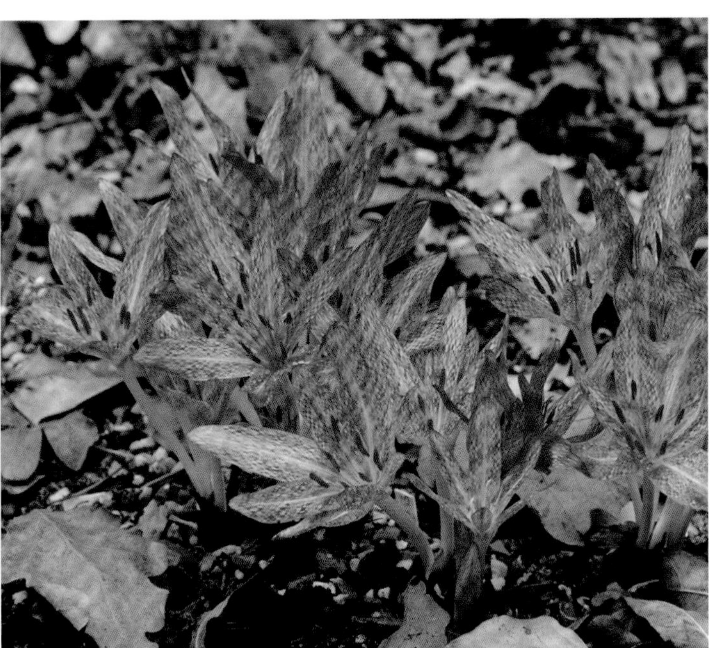

3

Salvia yangii is a sub-shrub, an in-between plant, too woody in its stems to be thought of as a perennial, but springing with fresh shoots from the base if cut down each season, like a perennial plant. It is a tall, upright beauty with grey-white stems and the same greyish bloom on the undersides of the leaves. It flowers in late summer and early autumn with long spikes of grey-blue flowers, the colour of catmint. It belongs to the sage family, and the foliage has that distinctive, aromatic sage scent. It makes a wonderfully misty setting for marigolds, set in a bright spread at its feet. These will flower for months during mid- and late summer, the earliest flush coming from autumn-sown seed. For a later crop, plug plants are usually available in quantity in spring. Marigolds are familiar, comfortable flowers, lovely to pick and very generous, lolling about surrounded by a mass of their own fat buds. Use the giant oat grass as the background here in an open sunny place, which they will all enjoy. Where it is happy, stipa will zoom up to 2.5 m (8 ft) in a season, producing long, elegant sprays of oat-like heads to sway over the brilliant marigolds below.

Salvia yangii 'Blue Spire' + *Stipa gigantea* / *Calendula officinalis* 'Indian Prince'

① *Salvia yangii* 'Blue Spire' (Russian sage)

HEIGHT: 1.2 cm (4 ft)

SPREAD. 1 m (3 ft)

FLOWERING TIME: Late summer to early autumn

STAR QUALITIES: Small flowers, massed together on the stems to create spires of soft violet-blue. Attractive, greyish foliage, intricately cut.

ALTERNATIVES: *S. yangii* 'Blue Spire' is the best of the selections from the species; 'Little Spire' is more compact, not reaching much more than 60 cm (24 in), but it is not as stylish.

② *Stipa gigantea* (Giant oat grass)

A native of Spain and Portugal, the foliage of this oat grass makes a dense, weed-suppressing clump about 70 cm (28 in) high. From this underpinning come elegant waving stems of oat-like flowers. When they first unfold, they are a purplish green, but as they ripen they gradually bleach to a soft straw colour. Though tall, they are strong and do not need staking.

③ *Calendula officinalis* 'Indian Prince' (Pot marigold)

Calendula's proper name comes from the Latin word *calendae*, the first day of the month, and is a tribute to the long flowering period of this common cottage garden flower. 'Indian Prince' is one of many varieties available, with a deep brownish-red flush on the backs of the brilliant orange petals. It is particularly lovely in bud. Marigolds are charming and easy annuals, flowering best in full sun. Regular deadheading prolongs the display. You can sow seed directly where you want the flowers, thinning out the baby plants as they develop.

(2)

(3)

This exotic combination requires some effort on the part of the gardener, but it will be worth it, seeing the season out with a dramatic flourish. The Mexican sunflower is an annual that looks like a perennial with its vigorous, branching habit. Started off from seed in spring, it will develop into a handsome plant up to 2 m (6 ft) tall, coming into bloom in late summer and lasting through into autumn. The flowers are rather like those of a single dahlia, each held stiffly on a thick stem that widens out underneath each bud. The colour is a rich orange, overlaid with red, salsa-like colours entirely appropriate for this native of Central America. The ginger lily grows from a fleshy rhizome and though by nature perennial, needs to be treated like a dahlia. In mild areas, if mulched, it might overwinter in the ground. Otherwise, it must be lifted and stored under cover. The most dramatic element of the group is the castor oil plant. Grow this from seed each spring to provide a background of superb dark, glossy foliage.

Tithonia rotundifolia 'Torch' + *Hedychium gardnerianum* / *Ricinus communis* 'Carmencita'

① *Tithonia rotundifolia* 'Torch' (Mexican sunflower)

HEIGHT: 2 m (6 ft)

SPREAD: 30 cm (12 in)

FLOWERING TIME: Late summer to autumn

STAR QUALITIES: Strong, tall presence and a succession of dahlia-like flowers in a brilliant, clear orange-red.

ALTERNATIVES: *T.* 'Fiesta del Sol' is a shorter variety (60–90 cm / 24–36 in), with flowers that are clear orange.

② *Hedychium gardnerianum* (Ginger lily)

Handsome lance-shaped leaves surround spikes of sweetly scented flowers, soft lemon-yellow in this native Himalayan species. The flowers clustering round the spikes have long red stamens that curl out like butterflies' tongues, making an elegant, airy display. *H. gardnerianum* is one of the taller gingers (1.5 m / 5 ft). *H. densiflorum* is more compact, with spikes of orange-red flowers.

③ *Ricinus communis* 'Carmencita' (Castor oil plant)

In its North African home, the castor oil plant is an evergreen shrub, but gardeners in cooler climates can exploit the fact that it grows fast and use it as an exotic, leafy annual. 'Carmencita' is tall (2–3 m / 6–10 ft), with dark bronze-red foliage that is far more important than the fluffy nubs of reddish flower. The colour is subtle, and the gloss on the leaf extraordinary, especially when set against other tropical-looking exotics such as the ginger. Handle with care, though: it is poisonous.

3

2

1

Strong dark pokerheads of *Pennisetum glaucum* 'Purple Majesty' in the Hermannshof botanic garden, Germany.
Alongside are the buff seedheads of *Amaranthus cruentus* 'Hot Biscuits' and zinnias, both 'Limette' and 'Profusion Apricot'.

ALTERNATIVE PLANT COMBINATIONS

In the preceding chapters, the star plants for each season have been given two ideal partners in order to create planting combinations that either provide a satisfying succession of interest through the year or, where flowering times coincide, an eye-catching burst of colour. These 'off-the-peg' planting recipes have been designed to suit all sorts of sites and soils as well as all kinds of gardens. You may also find they inspire you to create slightly different schemes, tailored to suit your own particular needs or tastes and your own particular garden environment. The following lists suggest additional good companions for each of the star plants, arranged here in alphabetical rather than seasonal order.

Once you have introduced opium poppies (*Papaver somniferum*) into the garden, you will never be without them because they are enthusiastic self-seeders. Here they are growing with *Salvia* 'Amistad'.

Aconitum carmichaelii 'Arendsii'

+ *Actaea simplex* 'James Compton'
Aster amellus 'Rosa Erfüllung'
Dipsacus fullonum
Helenium autumnale
Helianthus 'Capenoch Star'
Kniphofia triangularis
Leucanthemella serotina
Macleaya 'Spetchley Ruby'
Persicaria orientalis
Phlox paniculata 'White Admiral'
Rudbeckia hirta 'Indian Summer'
Sinacalia tangutica (syn. *Senecio tanguticus*)

Actaea simplex 'Brunette'

+ *Aconitum carmichaelii*
Argyranthemum 'Jamaica Primrose'
Astilbe 'Brautschleier'
Darmera peltata
Dipsacus fullonum
Francoa sonchifolia
Iris pseudacorus 'Variegata'
Kniphofia galpinii
Persicaria amplexicaulis 'Alba'
Symphyotrichum ericoides 'Pink Cloud'

Allium schubertii

+ *Agapanthus caulescens*
Anemone × hybrida 'Honorine Jobert'
Artemisia stelleriana
Cerinthe major 'Purpurascens'
Eremurus × isabellinus 'Cleopatra'
Gladiolus communis subsp. *byzantinus*
Lupinus (blue)
Nepeta racemosa 'Walker's Low'
Nigella damascena 'Miss Jekyll'
Paeonia mascula
Papaver somniferum 'Lauren's Grape'
Iris (bearded)
Smyrnium perfoliatum

Allium siculum

+ *Aconitum carmichaelii* 'Arendsii'
Agapanthus 'Ardernei Hybrid'
Euphorbia seguieriana
Ferula communis subsp. *glauca*
Galtonia princeps
Geranium macrorrhizum 'Album'
Helenium 'Sahin's Early Flowerer'
Hemerocallis 'Chicago Royal Robe'
Heuchera micrantha
Hosta 'Royal Standard'
Iris orientalis
Kniphofia 'Barton Fever'
Oenothera lindheimeri
Paeonia mascula
Pennisetum orientale

Anemone × hybrida 'Honorine Jobert'

+ *Ageratum* 'Blue Danube'
Allium cristophii
Athyrium filix-femina
Crocus chrysanthus 'Zwanenburg Bronze'
Iris 'Purple Sensation' (Dutch)
Lamium maculatum 'White Nancy'
Lilium pyrenaicum
Salvia involucrata 'Bethellii'
Tulipa 'Abba'
Verbena bonariensis

Aquilegia vulgaris var. *stellata* 'Blue Barlow'

+ *Allium giganteum*
Anemone coronaria 'Lord Lieutenant'
Colchicum 'Lilac Wonder'
Dianthus deltoides
Dicentra formosa
Digitalis (white)
Ferula communis
Geranium 'Ann Folkard'
Hyacinthus orientalis 'Carnegie'
Iris (bearded)
Iris sibirica
Lupinus
Myosotis sylvatica 'Ultramarine'
Narcissus 'Ice Wings'
Tulipa 'Couleur Cardinal'

Arum italicum 'Marmoratum'

+ *Astilbe* 'Brautschleier'
Ficaria verna 'Brazen Hussy'
Fritillaria meleagris
Galanthus elwesii
Gentiana asclepiadea
Geranium cinereum 'Ballerina'
Helleborus × hybridus
Iris foetidissima var. *citrina*
Milium effusum 'Aureum'
Narcissus 'Cedric Morris'
Papaver cambricum
Polypodium cambricum 'Cambricum'
Primula vulgaris
Scilla bithynica

Asplenium scolopendrium

+ *Anemone blanda* 'White Splendour'
Asarum europaeum
Athyrium filix-femina
Carex oshimensis 'Evergold'
Crocus banaticus
Cyclamen hederifolium
Hosta crispula
Narcissus 'Jenny'
Polygonatum × hybridum
Scilla siberica

Astrantia major subsp. *involucrata* 'Shaggy'

+ *Actaea simplex* Atropurpurea Group
Asplenium scolopendrium
Cardamine pratensis 'Flore Pleno'
Iris 'Lion King' (Dutch)
Lagurus ovatus
Narcissus 'Saint Keverne'
Nicotiana alata 'Lime Green'
Primula vulgaris Barnhaven Blues Group
Pulmonaria 'Lewis Palmer'
Scilla bifolia
Viola riviniana Purpurea Group

Campanula lactiflora 'Prichard's Variety'

+ *Achillea* 'Moonshine'
Aruncus dioicus
Euphorbia palustris
Galega orientalis
Lavatera trimestris 'Mont Blanc'
Lilium candidum
Lilium 'Casa Blanca'
Paeonia lactiflora 'Festiva Maxima'
Pimpinella major 'Rosea'
Tulipa 'Estella Rijnveld'

Ceratostigma willmottianum

+ *Cleome hassleriana* 'Helen Campbell'
Colchicum speciosum
Erigeron karvinskianus
Galanthus 'John Gray'
Iris 'Katharine Hodgkin'
Myosotis
Nigella papillosa 'African Bride'
Stipa tenuissima
Tulipa 'Ancilla'
Verbena bonariensis

Cerinthe major 'Purpurascens'

+ *Allium carinatum* subsp. *pulchellum*
Anemone coronaria 'The Admiral'
Camassia leichtlinii
Crocus chrysanthus 'Cream Beauty'
Fritillaria persica 'Adiyaman'
Gladiolus communis subsp. *byzantinus*
Hordeum jubatum
Iris 'Tiger's Eye' (Dutch)
Narcissus 'Double Campernelle'
Osteospermum 'Buttermilk'
Smyrnium perfoliatum

Cistus × *cyprius*

\+ *Cosmos bipinnatus*
Cynara cardunculus
Hesperantha coccinea
Lobelia × *speciosa* 'Dark Crusader'
Papaver rhoeas Mother of Pearl Group
Pennisetum alopecuroides 'Hameln'
Salvia farinacea 'Victoria'
Triteleia laxa 'Corrina'
Tulipa saxatilis 'Lilac Wonder'
Zinnia 'Queen Lime Red'

Corylopsis pauciflora

\+ *Anemone blanda* 'Ingramii'
Daphne odora
Galanthus 'Trumps'
Galium odoratum
Helleborus × *hybridus*
Hosta undulata var. *univittata*
Hyacinthoides non-scripta
Lilium 'Rosemary North'
Narcissus 'Hawera'
Pulmonaria saccharata

Crocosmia 'Hellfire'

\+ *Allium cristophii*
Artemisia stelleriana 'Boughton Silver'
Atriplex hortensis var. *rubra*
Bupleurum falcatum
Coreopsis verticillata
Dahlia 'Tally Ho'
Eryngium × *oliverianum*
Ficaria verna 'Brazen Hussy'
Foeniculum vulgare
Galatella sedifolia
Hemerocallis 'Green Flutter'
Kniphofia 'Nobilis'
Papaver commutatum
Physalis alkekengi var. *franchetii*
Sanguisorba tenuifolia var. *alba*

Cyclamen hederifolium

\+ *Anemone blanda* 'Ingramii'
Asplenium scolopendrium Crispum Group
Blechnum penna-marina
Corydalis solida
Crocus tommasinianus
Eranthis hyemalis
Erythronium californicum
Fritillaria michailovskyi
Iris reticulata 'Harmony'
Leucojum vernum
Muscari comosum 'Plumosum'
Narcissus 'Jumblie'
Ornithogalum nutans
Scilla bifolia
Triteleia laxa

Dahlia 'Magenta Star'

\+ *Amaranthus caudatus*
Arundo donax var. *versicolor*
Canna × *ehemanii*
Dipsacus fullonum
Iris 'Silvery Beauty' (Dutch)
Kniphofia 'Green Jade'
Ricinus communis
Rudbeckia occidentalis 'Green Wizard'
Salvia guaranitica 'Blue Enigma'
Symphyotrichum lateriflorum var. *horizontale*
Verbena bonariensis

Daphne bholua 'Jacqueline Postill'

\+ *Adiantum venustum*
Baptisia australis
Colchicum speciosum
Crocus tommasinianus
Cyclamen hederifolium
Helleborus argutifolius
Lunaria annua 'Corfu Blue'
Ornithogalum nutans
Paeonia emodi
Primula denticulata

Delphinium grandiflorum 'Blue Butterfly'

\+ *Crocus chrysanthus* 'Cream Beauty'
Hemerocallis lilioasphodelus
Iris reticulata 'Harmony'
Lilium Pink Perfection Group
Nigella hispanica
Paeonia lactiflora 'Lady Alexandra Duff'
Papaver orientale 'Aglaja'
Scrophularia auriculata 'Variegata'
Thalictrum flavum subsp. *glaucum*
Tulipa 'Exotic Emperor'

Dianthus 'Gran's Favourite'

\+ *Agapanthus campanulatus* subsp. *patens*
Anagallis monellii 'Gentian Blue'
Aquilegia 'Hensol Harebell'
Armeria juniperifolia 'Bevan's Variety'
Aubrieta 'Greencourt Purple'
Crocus chrysanthus 'Cream Beauty'
Gladiolus murielae
Lagurus ovatus
Phlox douglasii 'Boothman's Variety'
Triteleia laxa 'Koningin Fabiola'
Tulipa undulatifolia

Dryopteris wallichiana

\+ *Asarum europaeum*
Asplenium scolopendrium
Athyrium niponicum var. *pictum*
Begonia grandis subsp. *evansiana*
Cyrtomium falcatum
Galanthus 'Magnet'
Hosta sieboldiana
Matteuccia struthiopteris
Papaver cambricum
Polystichum setiferum
Pulmonaria saccharata Argentea Group
Saxifraga fortunei
Scilla mischtschenkoana 'Tubergeniana'
Trillium grandiflorum 'Flore Pleno'

Deutzia setchuenensis var. *corymbiflora* 'Kiftsgate'

\+ *Arisaema sikokianum*
Epimedium grandiflorum
Geranium 'Ann Folkard'
Iris 'Apollo' (Dutch)
Muscari armeniacum 'Blue Spike'
Myosotis
Primula beesiana
Saxifraga × *urbium*
Selinum wallichianum
Tulipa 'Greenstar'

Dicentra 'Stuart Boothman'

\+ *Actaea spicata*
Anemone × *hybrida* 'Profusion'
Colchicum 'Waterlily'
Cyclamen hederifolium
Euphorbia epithymoides
Gentiana asclepiadea
Gladiolus tristis
Glaucidium palmatum
Kirengeshoma palmata
Lilium apertum
Lilium formosanum
Milium effusum 'Aureum'
Polygonatum × *hybridum*
Primula capitata subsp. *mooreana*
Primula 'Guinevere'

Eryngium giganteum

\+ *Anthemis tinctoria* 'E. C. Buxton'
Asphodeline liburnica
Brassica oleracea 'Redbor'
Coreopsis verticillata 'Grandiflora'
Crambe maritima
Crocosmia × *crocosmiiflora* 'Solfatare'
Geranium pratense 'Plenum Violaceum'
Gillenia trifoliata
Hemerocallis 'Stella de Oro'
Lychnis coronaria
Narcissus cyclamineus
Osteospermum 'Pink Whirls'
Phlomis russeliana
Romneya coulteri

Erythronium 'Pagoda'

+ *Ajuga reptans* 'Catlin's Giant'
Arum italicum 'Marmoratum'
Crocus cartwrightianus
Kirengeshoma palmata
Lamium maculatum 'Beacon Silver'
Matteuccia struthiopteris
Omphalodes cappadocica
Primula chionantha
Pulmonaria angustifolia
Scilla bifolia

Euphorbia characias subsp. *wulfenii*

+ *Asarum europaeum*
Bergenia cordifolia 'Purpurea'
Galanthus 'S. Arnott'
Helleborus niger
Helleborus × *hybridus*
Hosta 'Jade Cascade'
Iris histrioides 'Lady Beatrix Stanley'
Kniphofia 'Alcazar'
Miscanthus sinensis 'Adagio'
Narcissus 'Geranium'
Romneya coulteri
Rudbeckia laciniata 'Herbstsonne'
Salvia uliginosa
Tulipa 'Cairo'

Euphorbia myrsinites

+ *Antirrhinum majus* 'Black Prince'
Bergenia stracheyi
Campanula portenschlagiana
Crocus angustifolius
Eryngium bourgatii
Lamium maculatum
Milium effusum 'Aureum'
Persicaria virginiana 'Painter's Palette'
Scilla bifolia
Tulipa 'Très Chic'

Exochorda × *macrantha* 'The Bride'

+ *Aquilegia* 'Hensol Harebell'
Cyclamen coum
Daphne 'Eternal Fragrance'
Dicentra formosa 'Langtrees'
Epimedium 'Jean O'Neill'
Geranium 'Anne Thomson'
Hepatica nobilis
Lilium pyrenaicum
Matteuccia struthiopteris
Sisyrinchium striatum

Fuchsia magellanica

+ *Campanula glomerata* 'Superba'
Crocus chrysanthus 'Cream Beauty'
Dahlia 'Bishop of Canterbury'
Iris 'Hildegarde' (Dutch)
Lagurus ovatus
Muscari armeniacum 'Blue Spike'
Papaver 'Patty's Plum'
Pennisetum villosum
Primula beesiana
Salvia involucrata 'Bethellii'
Tulipa humilis

Geranium psilostemon

+ *Agapanthus* (white)
Allium giganteum
Anthemis punctata subsp. *cupaniana*
Anthericum liliago
Aquilegia vulgaris 'William Guiness'
Arundo donax
Crambe cordifolia
Crocus speciosus
Dicentra formosa 'Langtrees'
Eryngium alpinum
Iris (tall purple bearded)
Lilium pyrenaicum
Matthiola incana
Polemonium 'Lambrook Mauve'

Geranium Rozanne ('Gerwat')

+ *Allium caeruleum*
Anthemis sancti-johannis
Anthericum liliago 'Major'
Aquilegia 'Hensol Harebell'
Clematis integrifolia
Crambe cordifolia
Dicentra formosa 'Langtrees'
Eryngium alpinum
Gladiolus 'The Bride'
Hemerocallis 'Golden Chimes'
Hylotelephium 'Ruby Glow'
Iris reticulata
Lilium pyrenaicum
Ranunculus acris 'Stevenii'
Sisyrinchium striatum
Thermopsis montana

Helenium 'Moerheim Beauty'

+ *Aconitum carmichaelii* 'Kelmscott'
Actaea simplex Atropurpurea Group
Amaranthus caudatus
Canna 'Durban'
Kniphofia rooperi
Lobelia × speciosa 'Dark Crusader'
Macleaya cordata
Physalis alkekengi var. *franchetii*
Salvia × superba
Stipa tenuissima
Tulipa 'Madame Lefeber'

Helleborus × hybridus

+ *Aconitum × cammarum* 'Bicolor'
Arum italicum 'Marmoratum'
Crocus 'Ruby Giant'
Epimedium grandiflorum 'Nanum'
Eranthis hyemalis 'Guinea Gold'
Euphorbia characias subsp. *wulfenii*
Galanthus 'Atkinsii'
Milium effusum 'Aureum'
Narcissus 'February Gold'
Primula frondosa

Hosta 'Krossa Regal'

+ *Anemone hupehensis* 'Prinz Heinrich'
Astilboides tabularis
Athyrium filix-femina
Echinacea purpurea
Filipendula rubra 'Venusta'
Helleborus argutifolius
Kirengeshoma palmata
Lilium 'Rosemary North'
Maianthemum racemosum
Phlox paniculata 'Le Mahdi'
Rodgersia pinnata 'Elegans'
Stipa tenuissima
Veratrum album
Verbascum chaixii 'Cotswold Beauty'

Hydrangea aspera subsp. *sargentiana*

+ *Anemone blanda* 'White Splendour'
Athyrium 'Lady in Red'
Corydalis flexuosa 'Père David'
Epimedium versicolor 'Neosulphureum'
Euphorbia amygdaloides var. *robbiae*
Geranium 'Bertie Crug'
Helleborus × hybridus
Hosta 'Francee'
Lathyrus vernus
Trillium sessile

Iris 'Jane Phillips'

+ *Allium hollandicum* 'Purple Sensation'
Crocus tommasinianus
Dactylorhiza elata
Eremurus stenophyllus 'White Beauty Favourite'
Euphorbia nicaeensis
Hemerocallis lilioasphodelus
Lamium orvala
Lamprocapnos spectabilis 'Alba'
Lysimachia ciliata 'Firecracker'
Symphyotrichum cordifolium 'Chieftain'
Tulipa 'China Pink'

Iris sibirica
'Flight of Butterflies'

\+ *Astrantia* 'Hadspen Blood'
Euphorbia griffithii
Francoa sonchifolia
Galega 'His Majesty'
Hemerocallis 'Corky'
Heuchera 'Raspberry Regal'
Hosta 'Frances Williams'
Knautia macedonica
Kniphofia 'Drummore Apricot'
Lathyrus vernus 'Spring Melody'
Lilium lancifolium
Mertensia virginica
Osteospermum 'Buttermilk'
Papaver orientale 'Cedric Morris'
Penstemon 'Alice Hindley'
Tulipa 'Bleu Aimable'

Lilium regale

\+ *Antirrhinum majus* 'Black Prince'
Campanula lactiflora 'Superba'
Cosmos bipinnatus
Delphinium 'Emily Hawkins'
Eucomis comosa 'Sparkling Burgundy'
Paeonia cambessedesii
Phlox paniculata 'Eventide'
Polemonium foliosissimum
Primula florindae
Tulipa 'Alfred Cortot'
Veratrum nigrum

Luma apiculata
'Glanleam Gold'

\+ *Anemone pulsatilla*
Armeria maritima 'Alba'
Baptisia australis
Cerinthe major 'Purpurascens'
Echinops ritro
Iris tuberosa
Myosotis sylvatica
Narcissus 'Geranium'
Salvia rosmarinus 'Severn Sea'
Tulipa linifolia 'Bronze Charm'
Verbascum olympicum

Mahonia × media
'Lionel Fortescue'

\+ *Anthericum liliago*
Galanthus 'Trumps'
Geranium 'Johnson's Blue'
Hedera helix
Helleborus × hybridus
Lunaria annua
Matteuccia struthiopteris
Narcissus 'Baby Moon'
Scilla bithynica
Smyrnium perfoliatum

***Narcissus* 'Quail'**

\+ *Athyrium nipponicum* var. *pictum*
Danae racemosa
Doronicum orientale
Eryngium alpinum 'Blue Star'
Erythronium californicum 'White Beauty'
Helleborus argutifolius
Hemerocallis 'Always Afternoon'
Hyacinthus orientalis 'Delft Blue'
Iris histrioides 'Major'
Romneya coulteri
Tulipa montana
Veronica umbrosa 'Georgia Blue'
Viola 'Aspasia'

Nigella damascena
'Miss Jekyll'

\+ *Alchemilla mollis*
Allium cristophii
Eryngium bourgatii 'Oxford Blue'
Erysimum cheiri 'Bloody Warrior'
Geranium wallichianum 'Buxton's Variety'
Iris (bearded)
Lagurus ovatus
Nicotiana 'Lime Green'
Papaver cambricum
Papaver somniferum 'Lauren's Grape'
Zinnia elegans 'Benary's Giant Lime'

Osmunda regalis

\+ *Arum italicum* subsp. *italicum* 'Marmoratum'
Astilboides tabularis
Caltha palustris 'Flore Pleno'
Carex oshimensis 'Evergold'
Corydalis solida 'George Baker'
Fritillaria meleagris
Galanthus nivalis 'Anglesey Abbey'
Hosta 'Blue Angel'
Iris pseudacorus
Maianthemum racemosum
Sanguisorba menziesii
Saxifraga 'Miss Chambers'
Trillium grandiflorum

Paeonia delavayi

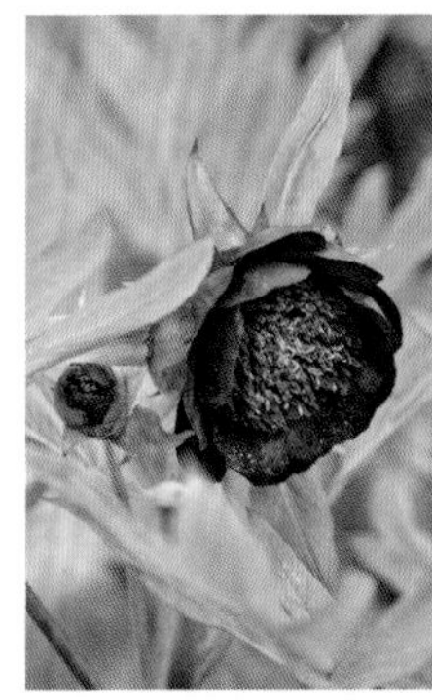

\+ *Agapanthus* 'Alan Street'
Digitalis (white)
Geranium Rozanne ('Gerwat')
Helleborus × *hybridus*
Hydrangea paniculata 'Phantom'
Lilium 'Casablanca'
Narcissus 'Thalia'
Pulmonaria saccharata Argentea Group
Saxifraga × *urbium*
Scilla siberica 'Spring Beauty'

Paeonia 'Love Affair'

\+ *Anemone* × *hybrida* 'Whirlwind'
Antirrhinum majus 'Black Prince'
Aquilegia vulgaris var. *stellata* 'Greenapples'
Camassia quamash 'Blue Melody'
Centaurea cineraria
Corydalis flexuosa 'Purple Leaf'
Delphinium 'Blue Dawn'
Fritillaria imperialis
Galtonia candicans
Gladiolus 'The Bride'
Narcissus 'Empress of Ireland'
Narcissus 'Merlin'
Saxifraga × *urbium*
Tulipa 'Blue Parrot'
Zinnia elegans 'Queen Lime Red'

Phlox paniculata 'David'

\+ *Astilbe chinensis* var. *taquetii* 'Superba'
Calamagrostis × *acutiflora* 'Overdam'
Helianthus salicifolius
Hemerocallis 'Marion Vaughn'
Iris 'Apollo' (Dutch)
Papaver rhoeas Mother of Pearl Group
Persicaria orientalis
Stachys byzantina 'Primrose Heron'
Tulipa × *gesneriana* 'Marjolletii'
Verbascum olympicum

Polypodium cambricum 'Richard Kayse'

\+ *Carex elata* 'Aurea'
Cyclamen hederifolium
Digitalis grandiflora 'Carillon'
Epimedium × *versicolor* 'Sulphureum'
Helleborus × *hybridus*
Hosta sieboldiana
Lamprocapnos spectabilis 'Alba'
Primula capitata subsp. *mooreana*
Pulmonaria 'Margery Fish'
Scilla bifolia

Polystichum setiferum 'Pulcherrimum Bevis'

\+ *Anemone nemorosa* 'Robinsoniana'
Bergenia 'Ballawley'
Carex elata 'Aurea'
Cyclamen coum
Galanthus plicatus
Geranium phaeum
Helleborus × *hybridus*
Hyacinthoides non-scripta
Leucojum aestivum 'Gravetye Giant'
Narcissus 'Hawera'
Primula alpicola

Rhododendron luteum + *Anemone blanda* (blue)
Arisaema costatum
Brunnera macrophylla
Chamaenerion angustifolium 'Album'
Colchicum 'Autumn Queen'
Convallaria majalis
Digitalis purpurea Excelsior Group
Erythronium dens-canis 'Old Aberdeen'
Polygonatum × *hybridum*
Polypodium cambricum 'Cambricum'

Rodgersia aesculifolia + *Acorus calamus* 'Argenteostriatus'
Actaea rubra
Astilboides tabularis
Galanthus 'Magnet'
Hosta 'Big Daddy'
Lysichiton camtschatcensis
Osmunda regalis
Primula florindae
Rheum palmatum 'Atrosanguineum'
Stipa gigantea
Zantedeschia aethiopica 'Green Goddess'

Romneya coulteri + *Agapanthus* 'Northern Star'
Crinum × *powellii*
Euphorbia schillingii
Gladiolus murielae
Orlaya grandiflora
Paeonia × *suffruticosa* 'Koshino-yuki'
Papaver somniferum
Salvia 'Blue Spire'
Thalictrum 'Elin'
Verbena bonariensis

Rubus 'Benenden' + *Allium siculum*
Anemone nemorosa 'Stammerberg'
Clematis recta 'Purpurea'
Erigeron karvinskianus
Foeniculum vulgare 'Purpureum'
Hyacinthus orientalis 'Hollyhock'
Nicotiana langsdorffii
Osmunda regalis 'Purpurascens'
Rodgersia podophylla
Salvia uliginosa

Salvia yangii 'Blue Spire' + *Alstroemeria aurea*
Eryngium × *oliverianum*
Euphorbia rigida
Iris × *robusta* 'Gerald Darby'
Narcissus 'Actaea'
Ornithogalum nutans
Phlox paniculata 'Eva Cullum'
Rudbeckia laciniata 'Goldquelle'
Symphyotrichum novi-belgii 'Porzellan'
Verbena bonariensis

Smyrnium perfoliatum + *Achillea* 'Credo'
Allium cernuum 'Hidcote'
Aquilegia 'Heavenly Blue'
Cerinthe major 'Purpurascens'
Epimedium pinnatum subsp. *colchicum*
Euphorbia griffithii 'Fireglow'
Geranium 'Johnson's Blue'
Gladiolus communis subsp. *byzantinus*
Iris 'Red Ember' (Dutch)
Iris × *robusta* 'Gerald Darby'
Limnanthes douglasii
Myosotis sylvatica 'Ultramarine'
Tellima grandiflora
Tulipa 'Spring Green'

Thalictrum delavayi 'Hewitt's Double'

\+ *Alchemilla mollis*
Catananche caerulea
Crinum × powellii
Geranium sanguineum
Gypsophila paniculata 'Bristol Fairy'
Helleborus × hybridus
Iris 'Blue Magic' (Dutch)
Iris orientalis
Pulmonaria 'Margery Fish'
Tulipa 'Amazone'

Tithonia rotundifolia 'Torch'

\+ *Asplenium scolopendrium* Crispum Group
Crocosmia 'Hellfire'
Dahlia 'Happy Halloween'
Deschampsia cespitosa 'Goldtau'
Helianthus annuus 'Claret'
Hemerocallis 'Corky'
Iris sibirica 'Flight of Butterflies'
Narcissus 'Sailboat'
Paeonia 'Bartzella'
Rudbeckia fulgida var. *sullivantii* 'Goldsturm'

Tulipa 'Prinses Irene'

\+ *Ajuga reptans* 'Catlin's Giant'
Bellis perennis
Doronicum × excelsum 'Harpur Crewe'
Eryngium giganteum 'Silver Ghost'
Erysimum linifolium
Euphorbia × martinii
Ferula communis
Glaucium flavum
Inula magnifica
Ligularia dentata 'Othello'
Lupinus
Myosotis sylvatica
Primula 'Guinevere'
Smyrnium perfoliatum

Tulipa sprengeri

\+ *Crocus goulimyi*
Euphorbia myrsinites
Fritillaria acmopetala
Geranium cinereum 'Ballerina'
Hosta Tardiana Group
Iris 'Black Gamecock'
Primula Gold-laced Group
Primula 'Wanda'
Pulsatilla vulgaris
Tellima grandiflora

Viola 'Ardross Gem'

\+ *Alchemilla mollis*
Ajuga reptans
Anemone blanda 'White Splendour'
Aquilegia vulgaris 'Nivea'
Arenaria montana
Aster alpinus
Carex elata 'Aurea'
Crocus sieberi 'Hubert Edelsten'
Geum montanum
× *Heucherella alba* 'Bridget Bloom'
Hosta sieboldiana
Iris 'Frans Hals' (Dutch)
Verbascum phoeniceum

Zantedeschia aethiopica 'Crowborough'

\+ *Angelica archangelica*
Astilbe 'Sprite'
Brunnera macrophylla 'Hadspen Cream'
Carex elata 'Aurea'
Iris orientalis
Ligularia przewalskii
Lilium 'Kushi Maya'
Lysichiton camtschatcensis
Osmunda regalis
Primula florindae

INDEX

Page numbers in *italics* refer to illustrations

H

I

J

K

L

M

T

V

W

Y

Z

ACKNOWLEDGEMENTS

Making a book is a collaborative process and writing is only the start of it. I have been extraordinarily lucky to work at Phaidon with an editor, Victoria Clarke, who has the unusual ability to recognize and resolve important details while never losing sight of the bigger picture. Her energy and commitment were astounding and I am very grateful to her. Because of the strange times we were all living through, I never met any of the people working on the book, but from Spain, the designer Paco Lacasta sent a clear vision of the way it should look, and Jennifer Veall undertook the massive task of getting in the very best pictures to use in it. Thanks are also due to the editorial assistant, Caitlin Arnell Argles, to the copyeditor, Diane Fortenberry and to Adela Cory, who was in charge of production. I'd also like to thank Clare Churly for proofreading the book and Vanessa Bird for compiling the index.

Michel Beauvais translated the text for the French edition of the book and it was put together by Baptiste Roque-Genest and Hélène Gallois Montbrun. I am most grateful to them for taking such care over the words.

At United Agents, my thanks are due to Becky Percival and Millie Hoskins.

Finally and importantly, I must thank Dr James Compton in the UK and Eric Hsu of Chanticleer Garden in the US for taking on the demanding task of verifying all the plant names in *The Seasonal Gardener.* They also checked that the pictures were correctly identified. I am very lucky to have had the benefit of their expertise as botanists and taxonomists.

PICTURE CREDITS

Alamy Stock Photo: Tony Baggett 145.1, 198tr, John Barger 175.3, Botanic World 151.3, Dorling Kindersley Ltd. 151.2, garfotos 153.1, 200cl, Frank Hecker 131.3, Miriam Heppell 143.2, Imagebroker 89.2, 143.3, Annette Lepple 65.2, mauritius images GmbH 177.3, Niall McDiarmid 29.1, 196cl, Christopher Miles 179.3, John Richmond 23.1, 141.3, 169.3, 183.1, 194tr, 199bl, RM Floral 71.3, 123.3, 151.1, 200tr, Steve Taylor ARPS 97.2, 183.2, Natalia Zakhartseva 153.3; © Richard Bloom: 11t, 19.2, 23.3, 25.1, 25.3, 31.1, 33.2, 35.2, 52t, 56-7, 79.1, 83.1, 93.3, 105b, 109t, 119.2, 125.3, 137.3, 141.1, 185.2, 194br, 197cl, 197cr, 199tl, 199cl; David Fairley Gardens: 129.1, 195tr; Dreamstime: James53145 79.3, John Caley 181.1, 198cl; GAP Photos: 171.2, Matt Anker 89.1, 200cr, Pernilla Bergdahl 135.3, Dave Bevan 127.3, Richard Bloom 75.1, 197br, Mark Bolton 145.2, Christa Brand 91.2, Jonathan Buckley 29.3, 69.1, 87.3, 91.1, 91.3, 147.3, 155.3, 179.2, 195bl, 200br, Jonathan Buckley - Design: Sarah Raven 127.2, 145.3, Torie Chugg 29.2, 77.2, 93.1, 201cr, Sarah Cuttle 67.1, 195cr, Frederic Didillon 33.3, 97.3, Jacqui Dracup 123.1, 193br, FhF Greenmedia 69.2, Tim Gainey 105t, John Glover 61.3, Marcus Harpur 63.3, Michael Howes 83.3, Martin Hughes-Jones 21.3, 33.1, 81.3, 135.2, 198cr, Ernie Janes 121.1, 193bl, Lynn Keddie 67.3, 127.1, 195tl, Geoff Kidd 85.2, Joanna Kossak 79.2, 97.1, 201br, Jenny Lilly 133.2, Robert Mabic 85.3, Nova Photo Graphik 31.3, 67.2, 123.2, 129.3, 131.1, 175.1, 194cr, 195cl, Abigail Rex 125.2, Howard Rice 75.3, J S Sira 63.2, 87.2, 183.3, Nicola Stocken 83.2, 129.2, Maddie Thornhill 21.2, Visions 121.2, 149.2, Visions Premium 59.1, 192cl, Jo Whitworth 133.1, 195br, Rob Whitworth 63.1, 93.2, 192br, Dave Zubraski 95.3; Garden Collection: FP/Arnaud Descat 37.2, FP/Frédéric Tournay 19.3; © Jason Ingram: 19.1, 31.2, 35.1, 37.1, 37.3, 69.3, 71.1, 73.1, 73.2, 77.3, 85.1, 95.1, 125.1, 155.2, 173.2, 177.2, 187.3, 193tl, 194cl, 196tr, 196cr, 198bl, 199br, 201cl, 201bl; © Andrea Jones/Garden Exposures Photo Library: 17, 27.1, 48-9, 61.1, 81.1, 87.1, 89.3, 112b, 117.3, 121.3, 139.3, 169.2, 181.2, 185.3, 187.2, 192cr, 196tl, 199tr, 200tl; Millais Nurseries: 27.2; © MMGI/Marianne Majerus: 153.2; © Clive Nichols: 9, 27.3, 65.3, 109b, 119.1, 133.3, 137.2, 143.1, 147.1, 149.3, 163t, 167t, 169.1, 171.3, 173.3, 175.2, 187.1, 192tl, 193cr, 197bl, 198br, 201tr, Jacky Hobbs 11b; © Claire Takacs: 12, 21.1, 23.2, 25.2, 35.3, 38-9, 41, 45, 52b, 59.2, 59.3, 61.2, 65.1, 71.2, 73.3, 75.2, 77.1, 81.2, 95.2, 98-9, 101, 112t, 114-15, 117.1, 117.2, 119.3, 131.2, 135.1, 137.1, 139.1, 139.2, 141.2, 147.2, 149.1, 155.1, 156-57, 159, 163b, 167b, 171.1, 173.1, 177.1, 179.1, 181.3, 185.1, 188-89, 190, 192tr, 192bl, 193tr, 193cl, 194tl, 194bl, 196bl, 196br, 197tl, 197tr, 198tl, 199cr, 200bl, 201tl.

Page 9 Spring explodes in the garden at Pettifers, Oxfordshire, UK, with silver-leaved pulmonaria surrounded by primulas, both dark and creamy yellow. Hellebores add purplish tones in the background, with bright blue spikes of grape hyacinth pushing up between.

Page 41 The lovely Viridiflora tulip 'Spring Green' was raised in the late sixties, but has always remained a great favourite with gardeners. It gracefully enhances whatever companions you might put with it, here the magenta flowers of honesty, a sprinkle of smyrnium and an underpinning of forget-me-not.

Page 101 The bright yellow heads of yarrow (*Achillea filipendulina*) hover like miniature spaceships over a meadow of perennials which includes tall thin stems of *Verbena bonariensis* and white-flowered *Lychnis coronaria*.

Page 159 A branch of *Rosa glauca* hangs over a vivid display of *Dahlia* 'Magenta Star' at Gravetye Manor in Sussex, UK. Behind are strong spikes of *Salvia* 'Indigo Spires' and the buff seed heads of *Calamagrostis* × *acutiflora* 'Karl Foerster'.

PLANT NAMES, AVAILABILITY AND HARDINESS

It has been a busy time for the Royal Horticultural Society's Nomenclature and Taxonomy Advisory Group. *Gaura* has become *Oenothera, Nectaroscordon* has been shunted into the allium gang, and we have been told to look upon both *Perovskia* and *Rosmarinus* as salvias. In *The Seasonal Gardener* we have done our best to keep up with the committee, but inevitably in the hiatus between writing and publishing, they will have had more opinions that will not be reflected here. Gardeners, of course, will continue to use the names they have always used. Not call a rosemary, rosemary? Impossible! And although it may have been a mistake to call *Scilla siberica* a Siberian squill, since it comes from Iran, that is the name under which you will find it in bulb catalogues, so we have continued to use it here. Common names of plants are those recognized in the *RHS A–Z Encyclopedia of Garden Plants*.

The availability of plants mentioned in the book was checked just before it went to press; inevitably, however, a few varieties may no longer be obtainable by the time you are reading. Plants should be available through good nurseries that offer temperate-climate plants – those happy in the UK, northern and eastern United States, and Europe. Anyone familiar with the invaluable *RHS Plant Finder*, which has been published every year since 1987, with the exception of 2021, will know that new plants are added each season (more than 3,300 in the 2020 edition), while a few old favourites are allowed to drift off to the compost heap. The best, many of which you will find in this book, will always survive.

In the UK, gardeners have the great advantage of a generally temperate climate. We have coldish winters and warmish summers, interrupted occasionally by worse than usual frosts and short periods of drought. I garden in the southwest of the UK, generally considered milder than the rest of the country and a few of the plants that happily grow here might not be so comfortable in the east or north of the country.

In the US, gardeners are guided in their choice of plants by USDA hardiness zones which extend from 1 (sub-zero) to 13 (sub-tropical). On this scale, much of the UK is reckoned to be zone 9, with the southwest nibbling at the edges of Zone 10.

Phaidon Press Limited
2 Cooperage Yard
London E15 2QR

Phaidon Press Inc.
65 Bleecker Street
New York, NY 10012

phaidon.com

This revised and updated edition published 2022

First published as *Plant Partners* by
Dorling Kindersley Ltd., 2001 and 2004

ISBN 978 1 83866 398 8
ISBN 978 1 83866 519 7 (signed edition)

A CIP catalogue record for this book is available from the British Library and the Library of Congress.

Commissioning Editor: Victoria Clarke
Project Editor: Victoria Clarke
Production Controller: Adela Cory
Design: Lacasta Design

Printed in China